A BRIEF STUDY GUIDE
FOR THE
BOOK OF REVELATION

LEONARD QUICK, M. DIV.

ISBN 978-1-68517-964-9 (paperback)
ISBN 978-1-68517-965-6 (digital)

Copyright © 2023 by Leonard Quick, M. Div.

All rights reserved. No part of this publication may be reproduced, distributed, or transmitted in any form or by any means, including photocopying, recording, or other electronic or mechanical methods without the prior written permission of the publisher. For permission requests, solicit the publisher via the address below.

Christian Faith Publishing
832 Park Avenue
Meadville, PA 16335
www.christianfaithpublishing.com

All scripture is from the New King James Version (NKJV)

Printed in the United States of America

I lovingly dedicate this work to the love of my life, my wife of sixty-eight years, Betty Anne Burks Quick.

CONTENTS

Acknowledgments vii
Introduction ix

Revelation 1: The Unveiling 1
Revelation 2: Letters to the Seven Churches of Asia Minor 7
Revelation 3: Letters to the Seven Churches of Asia Minor 12
Revelation 4: The One on the Throne of Heaven and
 Those Who Served Him 16
Revelation 5: The Scroll and the Lamb 20
Revelation 6: The Breaking of the Seven Seals 24
Revelation 7: The Selection and Sealing of the Saints 29
Revelation 8: Silence in Heaven and the Trumpet
 Judgments Began 33
Revelation 9: Demonic Destruction 38
Revelation 10: The Little Book 42
Revelation 11: The Two Witnesses 45
Revelation 12: The Two Great Signs 51
Revelation 13: Satan Gave His Throne to the Beast 56
Revelation 14: The Fall of the Evil Empire 65
Revelation 15: The End of Mercy and Grace 74
Revelation 16: The Undiluted Wrath of God 77
Revelation 17: The Power and Personalities Operating
 behind the Scenes 83
Revelation 18: The Cost of Surrendering to Evil 87
Revelation 19: Quantum Worship 92
Revelation 20: The Millennial Reign of Christ (One
 Thousand Years) 98
Revelation 21: The New Jerusalem 108
Revelation 22: The Throne and the Eternal State Began 113

Revelation Glossary 119

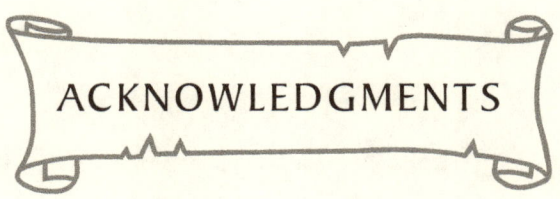

ACKNOWLEDGMENTS

I am grateful beyond words to my children—Terry, Glenda, Earl, and Gerald—for their patient contribution to this endeavor. I also want to thank my family who gave different levels of support and encouragement during the journey that produced this work. I am also indebted to Joan Hall Jackson for her diligent help in proofing and arranging this material.

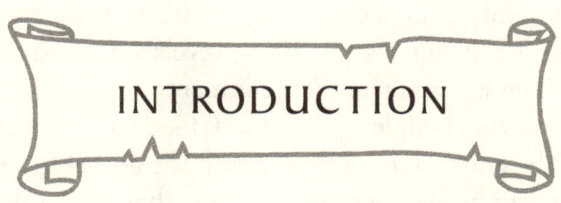

INTRODUCTION

The book of Revelation almost did not make it into the New Testament canon, which was closed between AD 365 and 385. The problem was that the eastern wing of the church, located in Constantinople, had a mindset that the western wing of the church headquartered in Rome did not share. In many ways, eastern thought did not always correspond with western thought. The eastern wing of the church found difficulty in believing that this document was the Word of God. This leads us to examine one of the most critical issues about this book.

The book of Revelation is written in what is known as apocalyptic language; hence, we speak of the book as the Apocalypse, which means "revelation" or "to reveal" in Greek. In times of stress and danger, ancient people, including Hebrew/Jewish people, resorted to a kind of coded language. In a world where the Caesars demanded divine worship—i.e., everyone was forced to worship them as gods—the young fledgling church could not afford to endanger its pastors and members nor its couriers. This type of literature made extensive use of hyperbole, symbolism, eastern exaggeration, grotesque images, numerology…and the list goes on. The most vexing problem for later readers is trying to decide what is to be taken literally or symbolically. The early church leaders were skilled in this language and were able to interpret its message for their members. That would especially be true for the eastern wing of the church where it was written.

Also, for greater clarity, I need to make mention of the way the book of Revelation is organized. Attention needs to be given to three cycles, vehicles, or waves of retribution, or divine punishment of sin. We refer to these as Seals, Trumpets, and Bowls. These cycles of retribution are not only designed to bring punishment for those insisting on following Satan but also to bring revelation, information, and vindication. The seal and trumpet judgments are designed to awaken humanity and bring people back to God. God spares no effort in trying to reach the entire human family with the gospel so that the need for judgment can be avoided. It is my view that the scroll seen in the right hand of the One Who sat on the throne contains the events that would make up the first three-and-a-half years of the seven-year, end-time period, which concludes human history on this planet. We will talk more about this later. No matter how difficult it is to clarify the message of the book of Revelation, we must make the effort. And this effort will most heavily depend upon the Holy Spirit to illuminate, guide, teach, and give us sanctified common sense.

Readers and students also need to be cautioned about the way the Revelation uses time, geography, and history. For example, as the student moves along at a steady pace, the scene changes abruptly in chapter 12. In chapter 11, we are on earth; but in chapter 12, we are in heaven. Likewise, we are not in the present tense but in the past. What happens in the opening verses is a veiled description of the "Christ Event," that is, the birth, life, death, and resurrection of Jesus. In this same chapter, time is greatly telescoped. What usually takes a paragraph is done here with very few words. All three of these movements take place within six verses. Be aware of these movements when reading and studying the Revelation.

It also needs to be clear that this document is not a commentary per se. It is a study guide for the book of Revelation. Among other things, this means that I will not comment on every verse or idea presented. With this in mind, I am allowed to select ideas, events, and passages with which the reader might not understand or be familiar. I am not a professional theologian, but I have served as a pastor for over fifty years. The most I could claim for this study guide is that it is a very important primer for the book of Revelation. My one hope and desire is that this effort will challenge and encourage people to take a new look at the Apocalypse. It is my hope that fear and uncertainty levels can be lowered so that many believers will have the strength to pick up their Bibles or this study guide, find a small group, and go on an exciting journey.

Before we leave this important introduction, two questions must be asked: Why did our Heavenly Father conceive the Apocalypse in the first place and pass it on to His Son, Who in turn passed it on to John? And why did our Heavenly Father feel the need to give His church this fresh and final Revelation? In my reading and study of the book, I have detected at least seven reasons, or purposes for the book to be written. Consider the following:

1. He wrote the book to inform the saints that one day all sin and evil would be banished from His universe.
2. He wrote the book to provide the church with a tool that would train and equip the saints for end-time living. This end-time living starts the moment the new believer confesses Jesus as Savior and Lord.
3. He wrote the book to mandate and encourage the people of God to carry as many sinners to heaven as they possibly could.
4. He wrote the book to assure His people that every question, both large and small, that has plagued the human race will be answered in full.
5. He wrote the book to convince the church that in order to go to heaven evil men and women must confess Jesus Christ as Lord and serve Him rather than strive for rehabilitation or reformation.
6. He wrote the book to show the church how to use agape love in the worst of conditions.
7. He wrote the book so that God's people would be ready to embark on their eternal vocations (heavenly work) when the Father and the Son declare it is time to begin this journey.

Undoubtedly in this equipping, the Lord will make use of our spiritual gifts as well as our special interests. I am not insisting that there are no other reasons. In fact, some of you may well find other reasons as you study the book. In addition, I greatly encourage every reader to be on the lookout for these and other reasons to appear.

Can this guide answer all our questions? The answer is no. Have I gotten it right in every case? Probably not. Are my views on key issues taught in this book satisfactory for everyone? Again, the answer is no. But one thing I do know is that this book is filled with hope for the followers of Jesus Christ. If there is one thing this world needs, including believers, it is God's kind of hope.

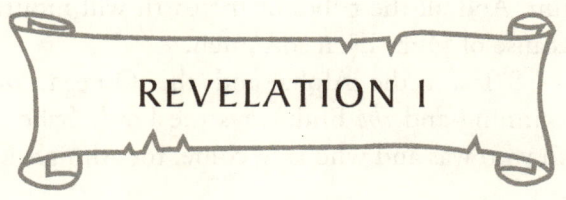

REVELATION 1

The Unveiling

1 The Revelation of Jesus Christ, which God gave Him to show His servants—things which must shortly take place. And He sent and signified *it* by His angel to His servant John, 2who bore witness to the word of God, and to the testimony of Jesus Christ, to all things that he saw. 3Blessed *is* he who reads and those who hear the words of this prophecy, and keep those things which are written in it; for the time *is* near.

4John, to the seven churches which are in Asia:

Grace to you and peace from Him who is and who was and who is to come, and from the seven Spirits who are before His throne, 5and from Jesus Christ, the faithful witness, the firstborn from the dead, and the ruler over the kings of the earth.

To Him who loved us and washed us from our sins in His own blood, 6and has made us kings and priests to His God and Father, to Him *be* glory and dominion forever and ever. Amen.

7Behold, He is coming with clouds, and every eye will see Him, even they who pierced Him. And all the tribes of the earth will mourn because of Him. Even so, Amen.

8"I am the Alpha and the Omega, *the* Beginning and *the* End," says the Lord, "who is and who was and who is to come, the Almighty."

9I, John, both your brother and companion in the tribulation and kingdom and patience of Jesus Christ, was on the island that is called Patmos for the word of God and for the testimony of Jesus Christ. 10I was in the Spirit on the Lord's Day, and I heard behind me a loud voice, as of a trumpet, 11saying, "I am the Alpha and the Omega, the First and the Last," and, "What you see, write in a book and send *it* to the seven churches which are in Asia: to Ephesus, to Smyrna, to Pergamos, to Thyatira, to Sardis, to Philadelphia, and to Laodicea."

12Then I turned to see the voice that spoke with me. And having turned I saw seven golden lampstands, 13and in the midst of the seven lampstands *One* like the Son of Man, clothed with a garment down to the feet and girded about the chest with a golden band. 14His head and hair *were* white like wool, as white as snow, and His eyes like a flame of fire; 15His feet *were* like fine brass, as if refined in a furnace, and His voice as the sound of many waters; 16He had in His right hand seven stars, out of His mouth went a sharp two-edged sword, and His countenance *was* like the sun shining in its strength. 17And when I saw Him, I fell at His feet as dead. But He laid His right hand on me, saying to me, "Do not be afraid; I am the First and the Last.

18I *am* He who lives, and was dead, and behold, I am alive forevermore. Amen. And I have the keys of Hades and of Death. 19Write the things which you have seen, and the things which are, and the things which will take place after this. 20The mystery of the seven stars which you saw in My right hand, and the seven golden lampstands: The seven stars are the angels of the seven churches, and the seven lampstands which you saw are the seven churches.

The Source and Origin of the Revelation

God the Father is the source of the Revelation or "unveiling." The Revelation seeks to do two things. First, it seeks to reveal to the seven churches of Asia Minor their spiritual condition and their relationship to Jesus Christ. The second part of the Revelation is designed to reveal what is going on in the present and in the future world. God's plan for the ages has always involved the church. This means the role of the church is critical in every generation. The Father gave this revelation to His Son, the Son gave it to His servant John, and John gave it to the seven churches of Asia Minor. Those seven churches in the first century represent all Christian churches of all time, meaning that God has given this revelation to each church today.

The Purpose of the Revelation

The purpose of the Revelation is to inform, train, and prepare each believer and church to understand and engage its culture as it is affected by the ongoing dynamics of the end times.

The Elements of the Revelation

- *The Messiah*: The Father had several choices about what the Messiah would look like and which version of the Messiah John would see and meet. He could have revealed Him as

the "gentle Jesus, meek and mild." He could have revealed Him as the risen Christ Whom the disciples saw in the first resurrection morning. But instead He revealed Him as the victorious Messiah Who was awesome in every way. His eyes were like flaming torches. His body resembled polished brass, and His feet and legs resembled the strength of bronze.
- *The Holy Spirit*: The key element to any revelation to the church is the Holy Spirit, without Whom the church could not survive, have any power, or affect the world.
- *The Lampstands*: The Lampstands symbolize the seven churches of Asia Minor. The primary focus of the church is to share the marvelous light of the gospel of Christ; hence, they are symbolized by lampstands.
- *The Stars and Angels*: Both of these names refer to the pastors of these churches. Why is the term *angels* used to refer to the pastors? Because angels are bringers of God's message to the church. Pastors bring the good news of the gospel to the church and to the world.

The Promise of the Revelation

Revelation 1:3 (NKJV) gives a promise to the person and/or church that reads, hears, and takes to heart (meaning takes seriously) the words of this book. That promise is the gift of wisdom, which means the ability to understand what one is reading and experience peace about whatever is happening and the power to not just endure but to flourish in a culture that seems to be coming apart. This is a warm invitation from God Himself to not fear and ignore this very important book but to spend time with it and embrace it. As you do, you will begin to hear the voice and feel the heartbeat of the living Lord of the universe Who is in the process of bringing history to a close.

A Critical Statement of Connection

In the light of all that I have written thus far, it is incumbent upon me, the writer, to make a critical statement about the connection of the letters to the seven churches of Asia Minor (chapters 2–3) and the rest of the book (chapters 4–22).

Two things: One, it is impossible to read and understand the book of Revelation and separate the letters to the seven churches from the rest of the book. The seven churches are not isolated entities but rather a collective body that represents all churches of all time. Two, the message of the Revelation was given to these churches of which we today are a part as we, too, prepare for, engage, and thrive in these last days.

The Apostle John (the Setting)

The apostle John was exiled on the island of Patmos off the coast of Asia Minor (modern-day Turkey). He was there because of his witness and testimony concerning Jesus Christ and the Word of God. He was "in the Spirit" on the Lord's day, and God sent a special angel to reveal His Word to John, who was prepared to listen and to write it all down. John wrote in about 100 AD.

The Sovereign Christ

Up to this point, the young churches and Christians everywhere thought of Jesus in His earthly ministry. Something then changes in this first chapter. Now they must think of Him and relate to Him as the sovereign Christ. First of all, His appearance was different, and so were His actions. We are told that His hair was white as snow, His eyes burned like torches, and His feet were as strong as brass. He was standing among seven lampstands and was holding seven angels and seven stars in His strong right hand. The lampstands represent the seven churches of Asia Minor, and the seven angels and seven stars represent the pastors of the seven churches. The seven spirits before the throne represent the Holy Spirit (Revelation 1:4). In fact, the number *seven* is the favorite number in Jewish thought. It signifies completeness and wholeness. God and His people are complete and whole.

Discussion Questions

1. Who is the author of the book of Revelation?
2. To whom is this letter addressed?
3. Define and discuss the seven lampstands, the seven angels, and their significance.

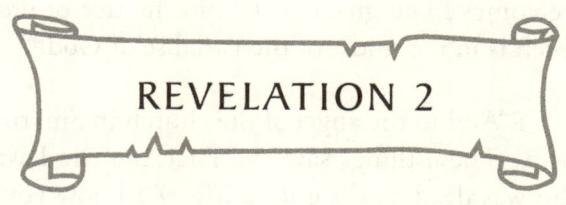

REVELATION 2

Letters to the Seven Churches of Asia Minor (Ephesus, Smyrna, Pergamum, and Thyatira)

1"To the angel of the church of Ephesus write, 'These things says He who holds the seven stars in His right hand, who walks in the midst of the seven golden lampstands: 2"I know your works, your labor, your patience, and that you cannot bear those who are evil. And you have tested those who say they are apostles and are not, and have found them liars; 3and you have persevered and have patience, and have labored for My name's sake and have not become weary. 4Nevertheless I have *this* against you, that you have left your first love. 5Remember therefore from where you have fallen; repent and do the first works, or else I will come to you quickly and remove your lampstand from its place—unless you repent. 6But this you have, that you hate the deeds of the Nicolaitans, which I also hate.

7"He who has an ear, let him hear what the Spirit says to the churches. To him who overcomes I will give to eat from the tree of life, which is in the midst of the Paradise of God.'"

8"And to the angel of the church in Smyrna write, 'These things says the First and the Last, who was dead, and came to life: 9"I know your works, tribulation, and poverty (but you are rich); and *I know* the blasphemy of those who say they are Jews and are not, but *are* a synagogue of Satan. 10Do not fear any of those things which you are about to suffer. Indeed, the devil is about to throw *some* of you into prison, that you may be tested, and you will have tribulation ten days. Be faithful until death, and I will give you the crown of life.

11"He who has an ear, let him hear what the Spirit says to the churches. He who overcomes shall not be hurt by the second death.'"

12"And to the angel of the church in Pergamos write, 'These things says He who has the sharp two-edged sword: 13"I know your works, and where you dwell, where Satan's throne *is*. And you hold fast to My name, and did not deny My faith even in the days in which Antipas *was* My faithful martyr, who was killed among you, where Satan dwells. 14But I have a few things against you, because you have there those who hold the doctrine of Balaam, who taught Balak to put a stumbling block before the children of Israel, to eat things sacrificed to idols, and to commit sexual immorality. 15Thus you also have those who hold the doctrine of the Nicolaitans, which thing I hate. 16Repent, or else I will come to you quickly and will fight against them with the sword of My mouth.

17"He who has an ear, let him hear what the Spirit says to the churches. To him who overcomes I will give some of the hidden manna to eat. And I will give him a white stone, and on the stone a new name written which no one knows except him who receives *it*.'"

18"And to the angel of the church in Thyatira write, 'These things says the Son of God, who has eyes like a flame of fire, and His feet like fine brass: 19"I know your works, love, service, faith, and your patience; and *as* for your works, the last *are* more than the first. 20Nevertheless I have a few things against you, because you allow that woman Jezebel, who calls herself a prophetess, to teach and seduce My servants to commit sexual immorality and eat things sacrificed to idols. 21And I gave her time to repent of her sexual immorality, and she did not repent. 22Indeed I will cast her into a sickbed, and those who commit adultery with her into great tribulation, unless they repent of their deeds. 23I will kill her children with death, and all the churches shall know that I am He who searches the minds and hearts. And I will give to each one of you according to your works.

24"Now to you I say, and to the rest in Thyatira, as many as do not have this doctrine, who have not known the depths of Satan, as they say, I will put on you no other burden. 25But hold fast what you have till I come. 26And he who overcomes, and keeps My works until the end, to him I will give power over the nations— 27'He shall rule them with a rod of iron; They shall be dashed to pieces like the potter's vessels'—as I also have received from My Father; 28and I will give him the morning star.

29"He who has an ear, let him hear what the Spirit says to the churches.'"

- Ephesus: The church that left its "first love." This first love refers to their joyful commitment and obedience to Christ. It speaks of their passion to bring people to Christ by living out and verbally sharing their faith with others. They were commanded to repent and return to their first love, or else Christ would remove their lampstand (the term *lampstand* symbolizes the entire church at Ephesus). The members at Ephesus hated the teaching of the Nicolaitans. This was a heretical group in the church that followed a teacher named Nicolas. This man had been blinded by Satan and rejected the divine nature of Jesus Christ.
- Smyrna: The poor, rich church. The term *poor* here actually means "material poverty"—God knows that many churches are monetarily without financial means but are spiritually rich in His eyes. God will in fact supply each church's needs according to His riches in glory. This church was also about to suffer for their faith in Christ and would have tribulation for ten days, which means an extended period of time.
- Pergamos: The church near Satan's throne. Satan's throne in this case means the seat of the Roman cult. The Roman cult was the place where citizens came to pledge their allegiance to and worship the Caesars. Also, some of the members were charged with the crime of following the doctrine of Balaam, which included eating food offered to idols and sexual immorality (Numbers 25:1–3). These first-century Christians were teaching and believed that neither the worship of idols nor the practice of immorality could harm them. They "believed" they had been "liberated" from the power of Satan and were protected by the power of Christ.

The church also protected and defended those who taught this doctrine of the Nicolaitans. We have already spoken to this issue where Christ's deity was denied.

- Thyatira: The compromising church. This church had among its members an influential woman referred to as Jezebel, who also believed in and taught the doctrine of Balaam. Her actual name was probably not Jezebel. The Jezebel of history was the wicked and evil wife of King Ahab of Israel (1 Kings 16–19). The leading woman at the church at Thyatira was assigned this name because her character and actions replicated the life and work of the original Jezebel whose evil gift to Israel led them into the worship of Baal. Baalism, the leading religion in Canaan, worshiped the principle of fertility. Sex orgies were always associated with this religion. The warning came from the Lord of the church that unless they repented, she would become literally sick and her children would die (Revelation 2:22–23). The term *depths of Satan* was offered as an excuse to study the pagan religions around them and participate in religious sexual orgies (Revelation 2:24).

Discussion Questions

1. What was the first love that was lost in the church at Ephesus?
2. What was the cause of the suffering mentioned in the church at Smyrna?
3. What is meant by the term *Satan's seat* in the church at Pergamum?
4. Who is Jezebel, and what was her role in the church at Thyatira?

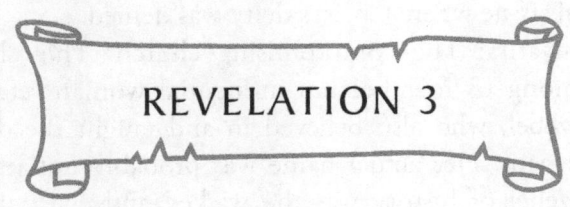

REVELATION 3

Letters to the Seven Churches of Asia Minor (Sardis, Philadelphia, and Laodicea)

1"And to the angel of the church in Sardis write, 'These things says He who has the seven Spirits of God and the seven stars: "I know your works, that you have a name that you are alive, but you are dead. 2Be watchful, and strengthen the things which remain, that are ready to die, for I have not found your works perfect before God. 3Remember therefore how you have received and heard; hold fast and repent. Therefore if you will not watch, I will come upon you as a thief, and you will not know what hour I will come upon you. 4You have a few names even in Sardis who have not defiled their garments; and they shall walk with Me in white, for they are worthy. 5He who overcomes shall be clothed in white garments, and I will not blot out his name from the Book of Life; but I will confess his name before My Father and before His angels.

6"He who has an ear, let him hear what the Spirit says to the churches.'"

7"And to the angel of the church in Philadelphia write, 'These things says He who is holy, He who is true, "He who has the key of David, He who opens and no one shuts, and shuts and no one opens": 8"I know your works. See, I have set before you an open door, and no one can shut it; for you have a little strength, have kept My word, and have not denied My name. 9Indeed I will make *those* of the synagogue of Satan, who say they are Jews and are not, but lie—indeed I will make them come and worship before your feet, and to know that I have loved you. 10Because you have kept My command to persevere, I also will keep you from the hour of trial which shall come upon the whole world, to test those who dwell on the earth. 11Behold, I am coming quickly! Hold fast what you have, that no one may take your crown. 12He who overcomes, I will make him a pillar in the temple of My God, and he shall go out no more. I will write on him the name of My God and the name of the city of My God, the New Jerusalem, which comes down out of heaven from My God. And *I will write on him* My new name.

13"He who has an ear, let him hear what the Spirit says to the churches.'"

14"And to the angel of the church of the Laodiceans write, 'These things says the Amen, the Faithful and True Witness, the Beginning of the creation of God: 15"I know your works, that you are neither cold nor hot. I could wish you were cold or hot. 16So then, because you are lukewarm, and neither cold nor hot, I will vomit you out of My mouth. 17Because you say, 'I am rich, have become wealthy, and have need of nothing'—and do not know that you are wretched, miserable, poor, blind, and naked—18I counsel you to buy from Me gold refined in the fire, that you may be rich; and white garments, that you may be clothed, *that* the shame of your nakedness may not be revealed; and anoint your eyes with eye salve, that you may see. 19As many as I love, I rebuke and chasten. Therefore be zealous and repent. 20Behold, I stand at the door and knock. If anyone hears My voice and opens the door, I will come in to him and dine with him, and he with Me. 21To him who overcomes I will grant to sit with Me on My throne, as I also overcame and sat down with My Father on His throne.

22"He who has an ear, let him hear what the Spirit says to the churches."'"

- Sardis: The living dead church. Sardis had a few members who had not "soiled their souls," that is, they had not compromised their convictions nor surrendered to these false teachers. Anytime we see white robes being worn by the saints, it is a reference to Christ's righteousness and the righteous acts of the saints.
- Philadelphia: The church controlled by brotherly love. God had set before the church at Philadelphia an open door. This door symbolizes both the opportunity and the power to practice powerful evangelism. This would be done by presenting the Lord Jesus Christ in all His redeeming glory. Also, the faithful in the church were promised to be kept or protected from a terrible trial that would come upon earth in the last days. This awful trial refers to that period in the end times when God would pour out His wrath on the

wicked (Revelation 16). In other words, these saints will have already been raptured and taken to heaven.
- Laodicea: The lukewarm church. There are vast numbers of lukewarm churches around the world, including America, that have closed their doors. These churches and denominations have compromised their theology and doctrines in order to be more acceptable to the present-day culture. Their lights have gone out. Their opportunities have been revoked. Their protection and power have been removed. Even though the church has lost its light, the compassionate Christ continues to appeal to lost people.

Discussion Questions

1. Concerning the issues at the church at Sardis, how would you define a dead church?
2. God seems to address problems and issues of each church so far. What were the problems and/or issues at the church at Philadelphia?
3. Define the term *lukewarm* in terms of church life today.

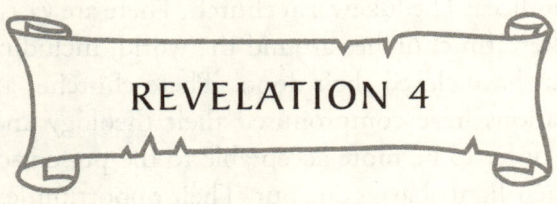

REVELATION 4

The One on the Throne of Heaven and Those Who Served Him

1After these things I looked, and behold, a door *standing* open in heaven. And the first voice which I heard *was* like a trumpet speaking with me, saying, "Come up here, and I will show you things which must take place after this."

2Immediately I was in the Spirit; and behold, a throne set in heaven, and *One* sat on the throne. 3And He who sat there was like a jasper and a sardius stone in appearance; and *there was* a rainbow around the throne, in appearance like an emerald. 4Around the throne *were* twenty-four thrones, and on the thrones I saw twenty-four elders sitting, clothed in white robes; and they had crowns of gold on their heads. 5And from the throne proceeded lightnings, thunderings, and voices. Seven lamps of fire *were* burning before the throne, which are the seven Spirits of God.

6Before the throne *there was* a sea of glass, like crystal. And in the midst of the throne, and around the throne, *were* four living creatures full of eyes in front and in back. 7The first living creature *was* like a lion, the second living creature like a calf, the third living creature had a face like a man, and the fourth living creature *was* like a flying eagle. 8*The* four living creatures, each having six wings, were full of eyes around and within. And they do not rest day or night, saying:

"Holy, holy, holy, Lord God Almighty, Who was and is and is to come!"

9Whenever the living creatures give glory and honor and thanks to Him who sits on the throne, who lives forever and ever, 10the twenty-four elders fall down before Him who sits on the throne and worship Him who lives forever and ever, and cast their crowns before the throne, saying:

11"You are worthy, O Lord, To receive glory and honor and power; For You created all things, And by Your will they exist and were created."

A Word of Caution

There are those who insist that in chapter 4 the church will be raptured at this point. They cite as proof that the word *church* is not used in the main body of the book after chapter 3. The solution to this problem is found in the choice that John made to write the book in the apocalyptic language. This language afforded some protection for the church, and as a result John chose alternate words. For example, his favorite term for the word *church* was *bride*, and in addition he used the terms *saints* and *those who wore the mark of God*. In fact there is no evidence that the church was raptured in chapter 4. However, there is plenty of evidence that this great event took place in chapter 14, verses 15–16.

LEONARD QUICK, M. DIV.

The Throne and the One Who Sat upon It

By God's command, the apostle John was instructed to come up to heaven. The first thing he encountered was the throne of God. It was a throne like no other, and immediately John was speechless, and words failed him. He realized that he was looking at the divine throne of God in heaven. He also realized that none other than the living God of the universe was seated on this throne. He made an attempt to convey what he saw by suggesting that the one occupying the throne looked like jasper and sardius gems. Although John made an effort, no language or words can describe God either in John's time or in our time. Keep in mind here that John did not actually look directly at God because the Bible teaches that no man can see God in the flesh and live. But the day will come when the saints of God clothed in their glorified bodies will be able to gaze upon His face as long as their heart desires. There was a rainbow around the throne that contained every promise that God had ever made to His faithful people, promises that He had kept to the fullest.

The Four Living Creatures

John encountered four living creatures in the middle of the great throne. One of these creatures had the face of a lion, another the face of an ox, another the face of a man, and a fourth the face of an eagle. These are strange creatures indeed! They are designed to represent every creature on the planet that lives and breathes. These creatures represent wild and domesticated animals, human beings, and everything that flies. Their main purpose is to lead in heaven's worship and bring praise and glory to the God of heaven. When the four living creatures offered up praise and honor to God, the twenty-four elders fell down before the throne and cast their golden crowns toward the throne where their submission and worship was obvious.

The Twenty-Four Elders

We are told that around the great throne were twenty-four thrones and upon these sat twenty-four elders. These twenty-four elders represent the saints of God in the Old Testament and the New. The first twelve represent the twelve patriarchs of Israel who were the sons of Jacob, and the remaining twelve represent the New Testament apostles. They were dressed in white robes and wore golden crowns that qualified them to be on their thrones because they had trusted the righteousness of the Lord Jesus Christ and they, too, had committed righteous acts.

Seven Flaming Lamps

These lamps symbolize the Holy Spirit. The Holy Spirit is symbolized in other ways, including the "Seven Spirits of God."

The Sea of Glass

In the ancient world, the seas and oceans represented chaos, turmoil, and unrest. In heaven John saw a sea not of water but of glass. This sea of glass in heaven tells us that there is no chaos, turmoil, unrest, or danger. In chapter 21, verse 1b, the Word says, "There was no more sea."

Discussion Questions

1. In verse 1, the apostle John seemed to have changed locations. The scene seems to change from where to where?
2. How many times is the word *throne* used in this chapter? Describe the one sitting on it.
3. What seemed to be happening around the throne, and what were those involved constantly saying?

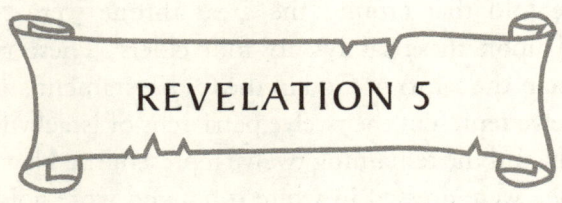

REVELATION 5

The Scroll and the Lamb

1And I saw in the right *hand* of Him who sat on the throne a scroll written inside and on the back, sealed with seven seals. 2Then I saw a strong angel proclaiming with a loud voice, "Who is worthy to open the scroll and to loose its seals?" 3And no one in heaven or on the earth or under the earth was able to open the scroll, or to look at it.

4So I wept much, because no one was found worthy to open and read the scroll, or to look at it. 5But one of the elders said to me, "Do not weep. Behold, the Lion of the tribe of Judah, the Root of David, has prevailed to open the scroll and to loose its seven seals."

6And I looked, and behold, in the midst of the throne and of the four living creatures, and in the midst of the elders, stood a Lamb as though it had been slain, having seven horns and seven eyes, which are the seven Spirits of God sent out into all the earth. 7Then He came and took the scroll out of the right hand of Him who sat on the throne.

8Now when He had taken the scroll, the four living creatures and the twenty-four elders fell down before the Lamb, each having a harp, and golden bowls full of incense, which are the prayers of the saints. 9And they sang a new song, saying:

"You are worthy to take the scroll, And to open its seals; For You were slain, And have redeemed us to God by Your blood Out of every tribe and tongue and people and nation, 10And have made us kings and priests to our God; And we shall reign on the earth."

11Then I looked, and I heard the voice of many angels around the throne, the living creatures, and the elders; and the number of them was ten thousand times ten thousand, and thousands of thousands, 12saying with a loud voice:

"Worthy is the Lamb who was slain To receive power and riches and wisdom, And strength and honor and glory and blessing!"

13And every creature which is in heaven and on the earth and under the earth and such as are in the sea, and all that are in them, I heard saying:

"Blessing and honor and glory and power *Be* to Him who sits on the throne, And to the Lamb, forever and ever!"

14Then the four living creatures said, "Amen!" And the twenty-four elders fell down and worshiped Him who lives forever and ever.

The Scroll

God is not interested in recording the great human events of history, even when they intersect divine events of the past. He is concerned about one thing, which is what is going to happen during the last seven years on this planet. The scroll was written on both sides and was held by the One Who sat on the throne of heaven. It was bound by seven seals, and no one was qualified to open it. This was probably the most important scroll ever seen by man. It contains the conclusion of human history and life on planet earth. This time frame concerning the last days is given to us by the prophet Daniel in the Old Testament (Daniel 8 NKJV). Daniel divided the seven years into two three-and-a-half-year sections. This scroll deals with the historical events that will mark the conclusion of human history. The roots of these historical events go all the way back to the garden of Eden. In Matthew 24, Jesus reviewed some of these events that would have their climax in the last seven years. He told His disciples that violence would be brought upon Jerusalem to the point that not one stone would be left standing upon another. We know this destruction happened at the hands of the Roman general Titus in 70 AD. Prior to this, the Greek leader Antiochus desecrated the holy temple in Jerusalem by boiling pig broth and pouring it over the temple floor. Jesus's rehearsal of some coming events did not carry with it any chronology. Only when Jesus referred to Daniel's prophecy concerning the last three-and-a-half years do we see the final chronological link by this statement: "The abomination of desolation" (Daniel 11:31; Matthew 24:15; 2 Thessalonians 2:3–4). The prophet Daniel, Jesus, and the book of Revelation agree on this point. This is why the breaking of the seals and the reading of the scroll is so important.

The Lamb

The only one qualified to take the scroll and read its contents, to John's surprise, appeared to be a lamb. (Also see John 1:29.) This Lamb had been wounded and killed in the past and now bears permanent scars. Did John see an animal with four legs? The answer is no. The person he saw taking the scroll was none other than Jesus the Messiah Who came in the flesh Who died on the cross as a sacrificial lamb in our place. What he saw was the resurrected Christ in His glorified heavenly body, scars and all. The emphasis here is on Jesus's total sacrifice.

Because of this, theologians of the past have declared that Jesus took our humanity back to heaven when He ascended. From this point on, for the most part, the Christ will be known as "the Lamb." The Lamb had seven horns and seven eyes, which are the seven spirits of God or the Holy Spirit.

Discussion Questions

1. What was in the hand of the one who sat on the throne? Describe it.
2. What caused John to break out and weep so profusely?
3. How was the problem solved?
4. What information did the scroll contain?

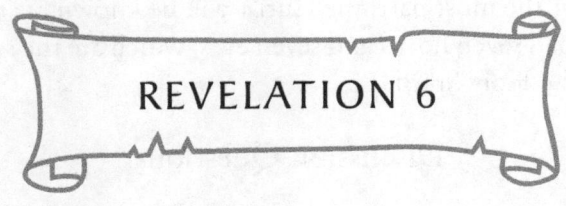

REVELATION 6

The Breaking of the Seven Seals

1Now I saw when the Lamb opened one of the seals; and I heard one of the four living creatures saying with a voice like thunder, "Come and see." 2And I looked, and behold, a white horse. He who sat on it had a bow; and a crown was given to him, and he went out conquering and to conquer.

3When He opened the second seal, I heard the second living creature saying, "Come and see." 4Another horse, fiery red, went out. And it was granted to the one who sat on it to take peace from the earth, and that *people* should kill one another; and there was given to him a great sword.

5When He opened the third seal, I heard the third living creature say, "Come and see." So I looked, and behold, a black horse, and he who sat on it had a pair of scales in his hand. 6And I heard a voice in the midst of the four living creatures saying, "A quart of wheat for a denarius, and three quarts of barley for a denarius; and do not harm the oil and the wine."

7When He opened the fourth seal, I heard the voice of the fourth living creature saying, "Come and see." 8So I looked, and behold, a pale horse. And the name of him who sat on it was Death, and Hades followed with him. And power was given to them over a fourth of the earth, to kill with sword, with hunger, with death, and by the beasts of the earth.

9When He opened the fifth seal, I saw under the altar the souls of those who had been slain for the word of God and for the testimony which they held. 10And they cried with a loud voice, saying, "How long, O Lord, holy and true, until You judge and avenge our blood on those who dwell on the earth?" 11Then a white robe was given to each of them; and it was said to them that they should rest a little while longer, until both *the number of* their fellow servants and their brethren, who would be killed as they *were*, was completed.

12I looked when He opened the sixth seal, and behold, there was a great earthquake; and the sun became black as sackcloth of hair, and the moon became like blood. 13And the stars of heaven fell to the earth, as a fig tree drops its late figs when it is shaken by a mighty wind. 14Then the sky receded as a scroll when it is rolled up, and every mountain and island was moved out of its place. 15And the kings of the earth, the great men, the rich men, the commanders, the mighty men, every slave and every free man, hid themselves in the caves and in the rocks of the mountains, 16and said to the mountains and rocks, "Fall on us and hide us from the face of Him who sits on the throne and from the wrath of the Lamb! 17For the great day of His wrath has come, and who is able to stand?"

The Breaking of the Seals

In the first century, official documents were rolled up (closed) and tied with leather strips. A hot wax seal was then poured over the knot, and a signet ring was impressed into the soft wax. Only someone with proper authority was allowed to break the seal and read the contents of the official scroll.

Here the only One qualified now broke the seals one at a time. He seemed to be in a hurry to break the first four. The following events that took place when each seal was broken would happen during the first three-and-a-half years of the "tribulation" period. When the first seal was broken, a white horse and its rider immediately appeared in John's vision. This rider was equipped with a bow but without arrows and was told to conquer without violence. My view is that this horse and rider represent the Antichrist and his final rise to power; he will use his magnetic personality to bring about a limited peace by consensus.

The second horse was red, and the rider was given a large sword, which depicts massive military violence and war to achieve a desired end. What he could not achieve by consensus he will achieve by military violence. The third horse was black, and its rider held a pair of scales, which symbolize famine, massive food shortages, and starvation. In better times a day's wages would buy eight quarts of wheat and twenty-four quarts of barley. In the end-time period, a day's wages will buy one quart of wheat or three quarts of barley. A voice from one of the living creatures shouted a command, "Do not harm the oil or the wine" (Revelation 6:6). This could mean that those who have the money could buy adequate oil and wine. But I think the better interpretation is that the Antichrist makes a commitment in his rise to power that the cost of oil and wine would be protected. It appears that God is saying He is aware of what He has promised and that there would be no changes. Oil and wine were basic staples in every Middle Eastern home. Therefore, these items must be protected. The fourth horse was pale, and its rider was death with Hades (Hell) following close behind. *Hades* is the Greek word for the holding place of the dead—in this case, the wicked dead.

The Small Group under the Altar

When the fifth seal was broken, John saw a small group of saints under the heavenly altar. These saints cried out for justice. They were given white robes and instructed to rest a little longer until the number could be completed by the same kind of death and violence they had experienced by martyrdom. They were given white robes, which represent the righteousness of Christ and also their righteous acts of living in faith while on earth. It is my belief that this small group of men under the altar make up the beginning of a special group that we will meet later in the Revelation. What we learn later is that those in this group had been violated and killed by beheading. It is no accident that they are found under the great altar in heaven. The altar is the place of sacrifice where lives are given, and it was only proper that John would find them there.

The Natural Order Fled

When the sixth seal was broken, the world was suddenly found in a state of convulsion. The sun was dark, the moon appeared as blood, and the stars were being moved from their places (possibly asteroid strikes and near misses). The prophet Joel alluded to this scene in Joel 2:31, and the Revelation describes it on several occasions. The One Who sat on the throne and the Lamb were so awesome and terrifying to look upon that even the elements of the natural order fled from their presence.

Discussion Questions

1. Many scholars believe that the rider of the white horse is none other than the Antichrist on his quest for total power. (Agree or disagree.)
2. He is told to conquer but is not given any arrows. This means that he will take over power by negotiation, but if this fails, he will use force. (Agree or disagree.)
3. This little group under the golden alter (verse 9) will make up the 144,000 when that number is complete. (Agree or disagree.)
4. What will be the purpose of this cosmic convulsion (verse 12)?

REVELATION 7

The Selection and Sealing of the Saints

1After these things I saw four angels standing at the four corners of the earth, holding the four winds of the earth, that the wind should not blow on the earth, on the sea, or on any tree. 2Then I saw another angel ascending from the east, having the seal of the living God. And he cried with a loud voice to the four angels to whom it was granted to harm the earth and the sea, 3saying, "Do not harm the earth, the sea, or the trees till we have sealed the servants of our God on their foreheads." 4And I heard the number of those who were sealed. One hundred *and* forty-four thousand of all the tribes of the children of Israel *were* sealed: 5of the tribe of Judah twelve thousand *were* sealed; of the tribe of Reuben twelve thousand *were* sealed; of the tribe of Gad twelve thousand *were* sealed; 6of the tribe of Asher twelve thousand *were* sealed; of the tribe of Naphtali twelve thousand *were* sealed; of the tribe of Manasseh twelve thousand *were* sealed 7of the tribe of Simeon twelve thousand *were* sealed; of the tribe of Levi twelve thousand *were* sealed; of the tribe of Issachar twelve thousand *were* sealed; 8of the tribe of Zebulun twelve thousand *were* sealed; of the tribe of Joseph twelve thousand *were* sealed; of the tribe of Benjamin twelve thousand *were* sealed.

9After these things I looked, and behold, a great multitude which no one could number, of all nations, tribes, peoples, and tongues, standing before the throne and before the Lamb, clothed with white robes, with palm branches in their hands, 10and crying out with a loud voice, saying, "Salvation *belongs* to our God who sits on the throne, and to the Lamb!" 11All the angels stood around the throne and the elders and the four living creatures, and fell on their faces before the throne and worshiped God, 12saying: "Amen! Blessing and glory and wisdom, Thanksgiving and honor and power and might, *Be* to our God forever and ever. Amen."

13Then one of the elders answered, saying to me, "Who are these arrayed in white robes, and where did they come from?"

14And I said to him, "Sir, you know."

So he said to me, "These are the ones who come out of the great tribulation, and washed their robes and made them white in the blood of the Lamb. 15Therefore they are before the throne of God, and serve Him day and night in His temple. And He who sits on the throne will dwell among them. 16They shall neither hunger anymore nor thirst anymore; the sun shall not strike them, nor any heat; 17for the Lamb who is in the midst of the throne will shepherd them and lead them to living fountains of waters. And God will wipe away every tear from their eyes."

The Selection of the Saints

Four angels who were charged with the responsibility of controlling the atmosphere in and around planet earth prepared to move. Another great angel from the east, however, instructed them to wait. John heard that this special number was achieved by selecting twelve thousand men from each of the twelve tribes of Israel. That complete number was 144,000 Jewish saints (Christians) who worshiped the living God and the Lamb. It is safe to say the small group under the altar in heaven was a nucleus for this completed number of 144,000 Jewish saints that would have a vital role to play in God's plan for the future.

The Sealing of These Saints

These 144,000 were sealed with the mark of God. From here on out, we will hear a great deal about men and women being "sealed" and "receiving the mark." This mark represents God's ownership, but what did it look like? Was it the sign of the fish (ICHTHUS), which when translated means "Jesus, Christ, Son of God, Savior"? Was it a tattoo of the cross on the forehead or a computer chip put under the skin? The answer is none of these. But the Bible does give us a clue and an answer. In chapter 19, verse 12, we are told that the Messiah had written on His robe a secret name only He and the Father know. In chapter 14, verse 1, we are told the 144,000 had the name of the Lamb (Jesus) and the Father on their foreheads. In chapter 22, verse 4, it says the saints had "His name on their foreheads." Here is our answer to the question, "What is the mark of God?" The mark of God in the end times is the secret name that Jesus the Messiah had written on His robe in chapter 19, verse 12, "that no one knows but Himself." This sealing (mark) symbolizes ownership and protection. We will learn later on that the mark of the Beast (the Antichrist) will be required of those who follow Satan. This deadly mark, or seal, likewise denotes ownership of Satan and the Beast. True to his nature, Satan will also have a "secret name" for each of his followers.

Discussion Questions

1. In this chapter, the 144,000 Jewish saints were selected and sealed. Why the number 144,000?
2. Why did the angel involved in the sealing come from the east?
3. What is the seal that the angel applied to the foreheads of the saints?

REVELATION 8

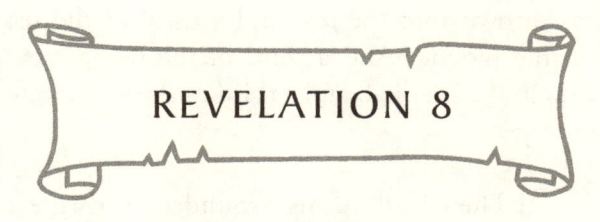

Silence in Heaven and the Trumpet Judgments Began

1When He opened the seventh seal, there was silence in heaven for about half an hour. 2And I saw the seven angels who stand before God, and to them were given seven trumpets. 3Then another angel, having a golden censer, came and stood at the altar. He was given much incense, that he should offer *it* with the prayers of all the saints upon the golden altar which was before the throne. 4And the smoke of the incense, with the prayers of the saints, ascended before God from the angel's hand. 5Then the angel took the censer, filled it with fire from the altar, and threw *it* to the earth. And there were noises, thunderings, lightnings, and an earthquake.

6So the seven angels who had the seven trumpets prepared themselves to sound.

7The first angel sounded: And hail and fire followed, mingled with blood, and they were thrown to the earth. And a third of the trees were burned up, and all green grass was burned up.

8Then the second angel sounded: And *something* like a great mountain burning with fire was thrown into the sea, and a third of the sea became blood. 9And a third of the living creatures in the sea died, and a third of the ships were destroyed.

10Then the third angel sounded: And a great star fell from heaven, burning like a torch, and it fell on a third of the rivers and on the springs of water. 11The name of the star is Wormwood. A third of the waters became wormwood, and many men died from the water, because it was made bitter.

12Then the fourth angel sounded: And a third of the sun was struck, a third of the moon, and a third of the stars, so that a third of them were darkened. A third of the day did not shine, and likewise the night.
13And I looked, and I heard an angel flying through the midst of heaven, saying with a loud voice, "Woe, woe, woe to the inhabitants of the earth, because of the remaining blasts of the trumpet of the three angels who are about to sound!"

Silence in Heaven

There is a time when God, men, and angels need to be silent. In fact, God says in His Word, "Let all the earth keep silent before Him" (Habakkuk 2:20). But what would cause heaven to go into a period of silence for one-half hour? Three things might be considered. First, the world had just gone through the seal judgment. One-fourth of the world's population had been killed, and one-fourth of earth's property had been destroyed (Revelation 6:8). In fact, there were saints newly arrived in heaven who came through suffering and martyrdom. They needed to be silent, to be focused, and to reflect on what had happened to them, their families, and the world itself. It is safe to say that our Heavenly Father was doing some reflection also concerning the extent to which the breaking of the seven seals had affected the human population on earth and made them sensitive to His presence, ownership, and worthiness. God and the Lamb must have been raising the question: Had hearts been softened on earth, and had men and women been drawn any closer to God and the gospel? How much more would it take to wake up the human race, separate them from Satan, and bring them to the Lamb so they could be included in heaven?

The second thing that would cause silence in heaven was the announcement that seven trumpets of judgment and retribution were about to be blown. This wave of retribution would be much more costly to the human family than the breaking of the seals. Maybe this second wave of destruction, suffering, and judgment on the human race would draw them to the Lamb. All that was about to happen when the trumpets were sounded would be very costly for God and for men.

A third thing that might cause silence in heaven was the prayers of the saints. We are told that the prayers of all the saints on earth would be mixed with much incense and that these would be offered up on the golden altar of heaven and its aroma would permeate the throne. When people pray, God listens and becomes silent. One of the most comforting things that could happen to those first-century saints who were reading the Revelation was to know that God was hearing and responding to their prayers in real time. That would be true for the saints of God in every generation, in every place, and in all times. Someone has said prayer is a hand that moves the hand that moves the world. The great angel who offered up the prayers of the saints on earth made an unexpected and strange move while at the altar. He took the sensor, filled it with fire from the altar, and threw it upon earth. And a great calamity broke out both in sights and sounds. Perhaps this was God's way of saying, "Turn from your wicked ways and loyalty to Satan and turn to Me quickly to avoid what is about to grip planet earth." It was almost as if God through His angel was saying, "Maybe this will get your attention."

The Trumpets Were Sounded

The breaking of the seals and the sounding of the trumpets take place in the first half of the last seven years of planet earth. After this the church will be resurrected from the dead and taken to heaven along with believers who are alive at the time.

Then the first trumpet was sounded by the angel, causing hail, fire, and blood to rain down upon earth. There is no way we can know exactly what these things mean now, but they certainly are instruments of judgment and retribution poured out on the wicked only and not believers. It is important to note here that the cost percentage-wise goes up from one-fourth to one-third here in the trumpet judgments. Can you imagine what kind of effect this will have on earth?

When the second trumpet sounded, something like a great mountain was thrown into the sea, and a third of it was turned to blood, which in a few days would create unbearable stench and odor. A third of the sea creatures were killed, which destroyed a critical food source.

When the third trumpet sounded, a star fell from heaven, contaminating a third of the freshwater sources. The star that fell was named Wormwood. As you can imagine, this water contamination caused massive illness, death, and chaos.

The fourth trumpet was sounded, and a third of the sun and moon were darkened as well as a third of the stars. These heavenly bodies began to literally power down by a third. It is hard to conceive the destructive effect this will have on the planet.

Discussion Questions

1. What was the purpose of the thirty minutes of silence in heaven recorded in chapter 8?
2. Is there a time when God needs to be silent Himself?

3. Is it possible that the judgment that occurred in the opening of the seven seals was designed to bring people to God and prevent them from taking the mark of the Beast? Explain.

REVELATION 9

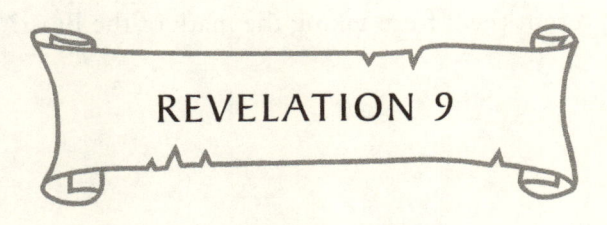

Demonic Destruction

1Then the fifth angel sounded: And I saw a star fallen from heaven to the earth. To him was given the key to the bottomless pit. 2And he opened the bottomless pit, and smoke arose out of the pit like the smoke of a great furnace. So the sun and the air were darkened because of the smoke of the pit. 3Then out of the smoke locusts came upon the earth. And to them was given power, as the scorpions of the earth have power. 4They were commanded not to harm the grass of the earth, or any green thing, or any tree, but only those men who do not have the seal of God on their foreheads. 5And they were not given *authority* to kill them, but to torment them *for* five months. Their torment *was* like the torment of a scorpion when it strikes a man. 6In those days men will seek death and will not find it; they will desire to die, and death will flee from them.

7The shape of the locusts was like horses prepared for battle. On their heads were crowns of something like gold, and their faces *were* like the faces of men. 8They had hair like women's hair, and their teeth were like lions' *teeth*. 9And they had breastplates like breastplates of iron, and the sound of their wings *was* like the sound of chariots with many horses running into battle. 10They had tails like scorpions, and there were stings in their tails. Their power *was* to hurt men five months. 11And they had as king over them the angel of the bottomless pit, whose name in Hebrew *is* Abaddon, but in Greek he has the name Apollyon.

12One woe is past. Behold, still two more woes are coming after these things.

13Then the sixth angel sounded: And I heard a voice from the four horns of the golden altar which is before God, 14saying to the sixth angel who had the trumpet, "Release the four angels who are bound at the great river Euphrates." 15So the four angels, who had been prepared for the hour and day and month and year, were released to kill a third of mankind. 16Now the number of the army of the horsemen *was* two hundred million; I heard the number of them. 17And thus I saw the horses in the vision: those who sat on them had breastplates of fiery red, hyacinth blue, and sulfur yellow; and the heads of the horses *were* like the heads of lions; and out of their mouths came fire, smoke, and brimstone. 18By these three *plagues* a third of mankind was killed—by the fire and the smoke and the brimstone which came out of their mouths.19 For their power is in their mouth and in their tails; for their tails *are* like serpents, having heads; and with them they do harm.

20But the rest of mankind, who were not killed by these plagues, did not repent of the works of their hands, that they should not worship demons, and idols of gold, silver, brass, stone, and wood, which can neither see nor hear nor walk. 21And they did not repent of their murders or their sorceries or their sexual immorality or their thefts.

Demon Locusts (Fifth Trumpet)

The fifth trumpet sounded, and demonic scorpions from the bottomless pit were unleashed on earth with the sole purpose of tormenting people who did not have "the seal of God on their foreheads." The demon scorpion attacks resulted in unbearable pain and agony only for unbelievers. To escape the pain, people would try to kill themselves but would be unable to do so.

The Demon Army (Sixth Trumpet)

John heard the sixth trumpet being sounded. The angel sounding the trumpet was instructed to release the four angels standing at the great Euphrates River. On the other side of the Euphrates, a vast two-hundred-million-man army was waiting. The size and equipping of this army will be entirely possible in the end times. This vast army was authorized to kill a third of the human population. Think about two things. That vast area on the other side of the Euphrates River had been the source of marauding armies that had devastated the people of God (Old Testament Israel) for centuries. Many military campaigns in the end times will be directed toward Europe and Israel.

Sadly, the fact and outcome of all this suffering under the trumpets did not have its desired effect. If anything, men's hearts grew more wicked and rebellious. What an awful and sad situation!

Discussion Questions

1. What is the purpose of the demon locusts in chapter 9? What group would they target for punishment?

A BRIEF STUDY GUIDE FOR THE BOOK OF REVELATION

2. The purpose of the awful punishment upon those who had the mark of Satan was a warning to those who had not yet taken the mark of the Beast. (True or false)

REVELATION 10

The Little Book

1I saw still another mighty angel coming down from heaven, clothed with a cloud. And a rainbow *was* on his head, his face *was* like the sun, and his feet like pillars of fire. 2He had a little book open in his hand. And he set his right foot on the sea and *his* left *foot* on the land, 3and cried with a loud voice, as *when* a lion roars. When he cried out, seven thunders uttered their voices. 4Now when the seven thunders uttered their voices, I was about to write; but I heard a voice from heaven saying to me, "Seal up the things which the seven thunders uttered, and do not write them."

5The angel whom I saw standing on the sea and on the land raised up his hand to heaven 6and swore by Him who lives forever and ever, who created heaven and the things that are in it, the earth and the things that are in it, and the sea and the things that are in it, that there should be delay no longer, 7but in the days of the sounding of the seventh angel, when he is about to sound, the mystery of God would be finished, as He declared to His servants the prophets.

> 8 Then the voice which I heard from heaven spoke to me again and said, "Go, take the little book which is open in the hand of the angel who stands on the sea and on the earth."
>
> 9 So I went to the angel and said to him, "Give me the little book."
>
> And he said to me, "Take and eat it; and it will make your stomach bitter, but it will be as sweet as honey in your mouth."
>
> 10 Then I took the little book out of the angel's hand and ate it, and it was as sweet as honey in my mouth. But when I had eaten it, my stomach became bitter. 11 And he said to me, "You must prophesy again about many peoples, nations, tongues, and kings."

Chapter 10 represents an interlude (pause) before the onset of the seven bowls of wrath. A great angel descended from heaven and stood astride the sea and the land. The sea is a symbol of chaos and turmoil and depicts humanity that is out of control, restless, and volatile. The land is a symbol of stability and order. The land in this case represents masses of people who are under some level of control and stability. The great angel from heaven indicated by his body language that he had a message not only for the apostle John but for the entire human race. He had in his hand "a little book," which contained the same message uttered by the seven thunders. A voice from heaven through the natural element of thunder spoke to John while he was about to write down into the Revelation the contents of the seven thunders and the little book. For now, he was instructed to eat the little book, digest it, and get ready at a future date to disclose its contents to the world. What John was told to do with the little book has nothing to do with eating but rather personal preparation to experience the message he was about to write. It is my belief that this little book contains a message about the last three-and-a-half years of human history and will express itself through the seven bowls of wrath poured out on planet earth.

What issues did John face at this point? Is it possible that God was unprepared to deliver the terrible message that John was about to write? Or had He forgotten something and was going back to correct it? The answer is no. God was not unprepared; rather, it was John who was unprepared to deal with the last wave of judgment the Bible called "the wrath of God." John was being asked to do something that no man, angel, or any other created being had ever been asked to do. He would have to prepare himself emotionally, spiritually, and physically. He would have to be prepared to see, hear, feel, and experience this terrifying message. Immediately the Holy Spirit and John's assigned angel began their work to prepare the apostle for this impossible assignment. The great angel standing on the sea and land raised his right hand to pledge and reassure the entire human race that God was in control of everything and that when the seventh trumpet sounded, the mystery (the work of God) would be finished, which He had previously revealed to his prophets (Amos 3:7).

> The seventh angel sounded his trumpet, and there were loud voices in heaven, which said, "The kingdoms of this world have become the kingdoms of our Lord and of His Messiah, and He shall reign for ever and ever." (Revelation 11:15)

Discussion Questions

1. Why did the great angel stand on the land and the sea?
2. Why was John not allowed to write down what the seven thunders said?
3. What does the eating of the little book on the part of John symbolize?

REVELATION 11

The Two Witnesses

1Then I was given a reed like a measuring rod. And the angel stood, saying, "Rise and measure the temple of God, the altar, and those who worship there. 2But leave out the court which is outside the temple, and do not measure it, for it has been given to the Gentiles. And they will tread the holy city underfoot *for* forty-two months. 3And I will give *power* to my two witnesses, and they will prophesy one thousand two hundred and sixty days, clothed in sackcloth."

4These are the two olive trees and the two lampstands standing before the God of the earth. 5And if anyone wants to harm them, fire proceeds from their mouth and devours their enemies. And if anyone wants to harm them, he must be killed in this manner. 6These have power to shut heaven, so that no rain falls in the days of their prophecy; and they have power over waters to turn them to blood, and to strike the earth with all plagues, as often as they desire.

7When they finish their testimony, the beast that ascends out of the bottomless pit will make war against them, overcome them, and kill them. 8And their dead bodies *will lie* in the street of the great city which spiritually is called Sodom and Egypt, where also our Lord was crucified. 9Then *those* from the peoples, tribes, tongues, and nations will see their dead bodies three-and-a-half days, and not allow their dead bodies to be put into graves. 10And those who dwell on the earth will rejoice over them, make merry, and send gifts to one another, because these two prophets tormented those who dwell on the earth.

11Now after the three-and-a-half days the breath of life from God entered them, and they stood on their feet, and great fear fell on those who saw them. 12And they heard a loud voice from heaven saying to them, "Come up here." And they ascended to heaven in a cloud, and their enemies saw them. 13In the same hour there was a great earthquake, and a tenth of the city fell. In the earthquake seven thousand people were killed, and the rest were afraid and gave glory to the God of heaven.

14The second woe is past. Behold, the third woe is coming quickly.

15Then the seventh angel sounded: And there were loud voices in heaven, saying, "The kingdoms of this world have become *the kingdoms* of our Lord and of His Christ, and He shall reign forever and ever!" 16And the twenty-four elders who sat before God on their thrones fell on their faces and worshiped God, 17saying:

"We give You thanks, O Lord God Almighty, The One who is and who was and who is to come, Because You have taken Your great power and reigned. 18The nations were angry, and Your wrath has come, And the time of the dead, that they should be judged, And that You should reward Your servants the prophets and the saints, And those who fear Your name, small and great, And should destroy those who destroy the earth."

19Then the temple of God was opened in heaven, and the ark of His covenant was seen in His temple. And there were lightnings, noises, thunderings, an earthquake, and great hail.

The Measuring

This is probably one of the most important chapters in the Revelation. John was given a measuring rod and told to measure the temple, the altar, and those who worshiped there. The term *measuring* in apocalyptic literature symbolizes ownership, identification, and protection. We see the Old Testament use of this term in Ezekiel 40:3. God owns the temple, the place where He meets with His people regardless of what we call it. No amount of suffering, hatred, and abuse can separate God and His people from each other. God owns the altar, the place where sacrifice is celebrated, where priorities are clarified, and where devotion to God reigns supreme. With this great teaching tool, God taught His people that without sacrifice, which involves the giving up of our lives, there is no way open to God. God owns the altar. The people who worship at the temple are God's people, and nothing can separate them from His plans and purposes for their lives. They bear the mark of God on their foreheads, and they can live under the promise of His protection. By protection here He does not mean to keep them from physical danger and suffering and even death itself. Rather, He means that nothing can separate you from His love and ultimate plan for your life. It means He will keep you from denying Him at the points of your greatest stress and suffering.

Then, when He is finished, He will bring you safely home, and you will be able to enjoy His peace and presence for all eternity.

The Gentiles

The statement about the Gentiles is a strange statement indeed. The apostle John was told not to measure the outside court because it belonged to the Gentiles. He was also told that the Gentiles would trample underfoot the city of Jerusalem for forty-two months (three-and-a-half years). But what does it mean? It means that in the end times, the first three-and-a-half years of the last seven years of human history on this planet, the Gentiles will have control of Jerusalem. Tourism and financial investments in Palestine and Jerusalem will be massive. Gentiles from all over the world will flood the land and the city. Everyone will want to visit the Holy Land during this period. So in this sense the Gentiles really will trample Jerusalem underfoot. But in another sense the Gentiles will control politically the ancient city as well. The Jewish leadership will allow the Gentiles to do as they please. All this will be allowed by the Jews for one reason. They will get their temple. The ancient Jewish temple that was destroyed by the Roman general Titus in 70 AD will be rebuilt on the ancient Temple Mount.

The Two Witnesses

We are not able to identify these two witnesses. Were they Moses and Elijah or another great Old Testament saint and the apostle Paul? We don't know. But we do know that these two men were Jewish believers who had been given a worldwide assignment to lead the people of God in a program of witness, testimony, and preaching the likes of which the world had never seen before. The scale and scope of this evangelistic outreach ministry reached around the entire planet. These men, along with thousands if not millions of other believers, were bearing witness during this period to every person on the planet. To enhance their witness and testimony, these two men and others in every country on the globe would be empowered with the ability to do miracles, mighty acts, and a fresh display of the awesome power of God. It was at this time and during this period that vast numbers of Jewish people would claim Jesus Christ as their Messiah, the Lamb of God. These two witnesses may correspond to what Paul was teaching and described for us in chapter 11, verse 26, of Romans when he said, "All Israel will be saved." It is also possible the 144,000 Jewish Christians (or saints) would be a part of this great campaign to reach the lost (Revelation 7:4). These new converts would join the Two Witnesses and work in their program of world evangelization.

These two men are called the "Two Olive Trees" and the "Two Lampstands" (Zechariah 4:11–14).

Above everything else, they would be sharing the light of the gospel of the Messiah with a broken world; hence, they are called lampstands. Light derived its energy, especially in the Middle East, from the olive oil taken from the olive tree. The olive tree here symbolizes the presence and power of the Holy Spirit in Jewish thought. These two men and those they led had learned how to depend completely and fully upon the power of God through the presence and personality of the Holy Spirit. These two men who headed up this worldwide outreach ministry had reached a point where the greatest thing they could do for God was to give up their lives for the gospel. This is exactly what they did! They were hated and despised by those who had the mark of Satan. Because of this, they were not even granted a decent burial, but their bodies were left lying in the streets of Jerusalem like pieces of garbage for over three days. But God had an alternate plan for their lives as He was about to raise them both from the dead before a watching world. "And they [the two witnesses] heard a loud voice from heaven saying, 'Come up here.' And they ascended to heaven in a cloud" (Revelation 11:12). God saves His best for all His people, and when their work is finished on this earth, He will call them home.

LEONARD QUICK, M. DIV.

God's Sovereign Rule

In chapter 11, verse 15, we are told that God's sovereign rule over heaven and earth reached a new level. In some ways the Revelation is a story of the conflict of sovereignties. The ego-filled leaders on this planet have maintained that they have sovereign (complete) control over their citizens. But the people of God know there is only one sovereign in this universe, and He is the Creator God Who has manifested Himself on earth as the Messiah. There is no other sovereignty. Because of this abrupt declaration in the end times—"The kingdoms of this world have become the kingdoms of God and His Christ and He shall rule forever and ever" (Revelation 11:15)—we are free to ask why this declaration was expressed at this time. One of the things I can tell us is that when Adam and Eve sinned in the garden, Satan took possession of all that they had legally. They were given by God Himself the right to have dominion and rule over planet earth and its environment. They had to surrender this dominion and rule over planet earth when they chose for themselves a new god and a new set of rules to live by. Jesus and Paul indicated that at present Satan is the prince and ruler of this planet. At the cross and through the resurrection, Jesus Christ stripped Satan of all of his power and rights. Why did God not declare at the resurrection His final and total sovereignty over the universe, including this planet? It seems that it would have been an ideal time to make that declaration. But man's ways are not God's ways, and there is so much we do not know and even more that we do not understand. When this declaration was made at this time, it threw heaven into a state of quantum worship and praise.

Discussion Questions

1. What does the statement mean when it says the Gentiles will trample underfoot the city of Jerusalem for three-and-a-half years?
2. Who are these two witnesses in chapter 11?
3. Discuss the two witnesses and the reference to them as the two lampstands and two olive trees.

REVELATION 12

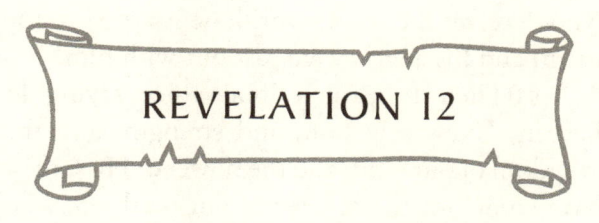

The Two Great Signs

1Now a great sign appeared in heaven: a woman clothed with the sun, with the moon under her feet, and on her head a garland of twelve stars. 2Then being with child, she cried out in labor and in pain to give birth.

3And another sign appeared in heaven: behold, a great, fiery red dragon having seven heads and ten horns, and seven diadems on his heads. 4His tail drew a third of the stars of heaven and threw them to the earth. And the dragon stood before the woman who was ready to give birth, to devour her Child as soon as it was born. 5She bore a male Child who was to rule all nations with a rod of iron. And her Child was caught up to God and His throne. 6Then the woman fled into the wilderness, where she has a place prepared by God, that they should feed her there one thousand two hundred and sixty days.

7And war broke out in heaven: Michael and his angels fought with the dragon; and the dragon and his angels fought, 8but they did not prevail, nor was a place found for them in heaven any longer. 9So the great dragon was cast out, that serpent of old, called the Devil and Satan, who deceives the whole world; he was cast to the earth, and his angels were cast out with him.

10Then I heard a loud voice saying in heaven, "Now salvation, and strength, and the kingdom of our God, and the power of His Christ have come, for the accuser of our brethren, who accused them before our God day and night, has been cast down. 11And they overcame him by the blood of the Lamb and by the word of their testimony, and they did not love their lives to the death. 12Therefore rejoice, O heavens, and you who dwell in them! Woe to the inhabitants of the earth and the sea! For the devil has come down to you, having great wrath, because he knows that he has a short time."

13Now when the dragon saw that he had been cast to the earth, he persecuted the woman who gave birth to the male *Child*. 14But the woman was given two wings of a great eagle, that she might fly into the wilderness to her place, where she is nourished for a time and times and half a time, from the presence of the serpent. 15So the serpent spewed water out of his mouth like a flood after the woman, that he might cause her to be carried away by the flood. 16But the earth helped the woman, and the earth opened its mouth and swallowed up the flood which the dragon had spewed out of his mouth. 17And the dragon was enraged with the woman, and he went to make war with the rest of her offspring, who keep the commandments of God and have the testimony of Jesus Christ.

Two Great Signs in Heaven

Chapter 12 is another historical interlude, which is a flashback to the birth of Jesus and the whole Christ event. The first great sign in heaven involves a woman who was about to give birth to a male child. She was clothed with the sun, and the moon was her footstool. This woman had a garland (crown) on her head that contained twelve stars. The woman represents the nation of Israel, or at least that special remnant in Israel that waited on the Messiah. The stars on her head represent the twelve tribes of Israel, the ancient people of God. After Jesus's birth, the child was caught up to heaven and to the throne. But even before she gave birth, a fiery red dragon stood in front of her ready to devour this child the moment it was born.

The second great sign is the aforementioned dragon, which represents Satan, the old devil himself. What we have here is an abbreviated form of the Christ event. At Jesus's birth Herod the Great played the part of the dragon, when he had all the male children two years of age and under slaughtered in and around Bethlehem. In chapter 11, the woman's adversary, the fiery red dragon, had seven heads, ten horns, and seven crowns on his heads. The number *seven* represents completeness and fullness. Satan is completely evil and has completely failed with every conceivable form of evil. The seven heads here represent seven kings or rulers and at times seven hills or mountains. The ten horns represent ten rulers who will be selected by the evil one who will have a part in shaping time and history. We will hear more about these heads and horns later.

The War in Heaven

In this flashback into history, we are told that war broke out in heaven between Michael and his angels and Satan and his angels. Satan and his angels were defeated and banished from having any further access to the throne of God in heaven, nor could they any longer accuse the saints of God on earth. Together they were thrown down to the earth where their revenge would result in destruction and violence throughout history. When Satan realized what had happened, he went after the woman with new levels of hatred and persecution. Keep in mind that "the woman" is symbolically the Jewish people who had helped bring the Messiah into the world. At first the woman fled to a place in the wilderness for protection for three-and-a-half years, or 1260 days. This tells us what takes place in the first three-and-a-half years of the seven-year end-time period.

Satan spewed out a deluge of water in an effort to kill her, but the earth assisted her by swallowing up the water. This deluge probably is telling us that new waves of hatred were released against God's people. Or it could be a form of military action. When Satan could not succeed against the woman, he went after her offspring, who were those who follow the Lamb and have a strong salvation testimony.

There are two things of special interest that are mentioned in this historical flashback. First, we are told that the Dragon threw a third of the stars in heaven with his tail and cast them down to earth. Second, we are told that one-third of the angels in heaven followed Satan and his great rebellion against God. These two passages are describing the same event.

We are also told that when Satan was defeated in heaven by the angel Michael, he was thrown down to earth. In Luke 10:18 Jesus announced to His disciples that He had just seen Satan fall from heaven like a bolt of lightning. These two passages are likewise describing the same event. Again, this means that Satan was banished from any access to the throne during the earthly life of Jesus even before the crucifixion and resurrection.

Discussion Questions

1. Who is the great woman who is discussed in the opening verses of chapter 12?
2. Satan does not literally look like a fiery red dragon. Is this language talking about his evil inner nature?
3. Where was this divine child born on planet earth? And what was his name?

4. In the war in heaven, Satan and his angels were defeated and cast out and denied any further access to the throne of God. Where does Satan and his angels dwell on earth now?

REVELATION 13

Satan Gave His Throne to the Beast

1Then I stood on the sand of the sea. And I saw a beast rising up out of the sea, having seven heads and ten horns, and on his horns ten crowns, and on his heads a blasphemous name. 2Now the beast which I saw was like a leopard, his feet were like *the feet of* a bear, and his mouth like the mouth of a lion. The dragon gave him his power, his throne, and great authority. 3And I saw one of his heads as if it had been mortally wounded, and his deadly wound was healed. And all the world marveled and followed the beast. 4So they worshiped the dragon who gave authority to the beast; and they worshiped the beast, saying, "Who *is* like the beast? Who is able to make war with him?"

5And he was given a mouth speaking great things and blasphemies, and he was given authority to continue for forty-two months. 6Then he opened his mouth in blasphemy against God, to blaspheme His name, His tabernacle, and those who dwell in heaven. 7It was granted to him to make war with the saints and to overcome them. And authority was given him over every tribe, tongue, and nation. 8All who dwell on the earth will worship him, whose names have not been written in the Book of Life of the Lamb slain from the foundation of the world.

9If anyone has an ear, let him hear. 10He who leads into captivity shall go into captivity; he who kills with the sword must be killed with the sword. Here is the patience and the faith of the saints.

11Then I saw another beast coming up out of the earth, and he had two horns like a lamb and spoke like a dragon. 12And he exercises all the authority of the first beast in his presence, and causes the earth and those who dwell in it to worship the first beast, whose deadly wound was healed. 13He performs great signs, so that he even makes fire come down from heaven on the earth in the sight of men. 14And he deceives those who dwell on the earth by those signs which he was granted to do in the sight of the beast, telling those who dwell on the earth to make an image to the beast who was wounded by the sword and lived. 15He was granted *power* to give breath to the image of the beast, that the image of the beast should both speak and cause as many as would not worship the image of the beast to be killed. 16He causes all, both small and great, rich and poor, free and slave, to receive a mark on their right hand or on their foreheads, 17and that no one may buy or sell except one who has the mark or the name of the beast, or the number of his name.

18Here is wisdom. Let him who has understanding calculate the number of the beast, for it is the number of a man: His number *is* 666.

In chapter 13, we encounter a crucial chapter in the book. In order to help us understand this chapter and better interpret it, please indulge me as I present the following scenario. I have chosen the scenario concept for more than one reason. It allows me more freedom in suggesting how a passage is to be interpreted. In fact, this concept will allow me to present my views alongside other existing ones.

Scenario 1
The Earth Crowned Its King

This chapter is a major division in the book in terms of chronology. The Lamb broke the seals so we could read and understand what was on the scroll. We have also heard the trumpet judgments. These two instruments unfolded in the first three-and-a-half years of the seven-year time period. In this passage, we are face-to-face with three of the most dreadful people in history. But how did history get to this point? The first Beast is also known as the Antichrist, the lawless one, and sometimes the man of sin. The term *beast* indicates that this person is a terrifying creature. This Beast began his journey to power long before what is announced in chapter 13. He probably started with the United Nations organization but soon realized that this would be too slow to propel him into world recognition and domination. It is my view that the Antichrist or the Beast persuaded Europe to create a fast-track organization that I am calling a Council of Regents and he soon became its indispensable leader. His mantra and the mantra of the council were peace, prosperity, and progress. This mantra soon made its way from the Internet to billboards and every form of media available that could get the attention of the masses. His accomplishments through the Council were nothing short of remarkable. Peace began to slowly return to Europe, and prosperity could be seen taking root. But the most remarkable place for achievements could be seen in the Middle East, especially Palestine and Jerusalem. The magnetic personality of the Beast had persuaded Arabs to do what everyone thought was totally impossible. They agreed to have the Dome of the Rock moved to a new location on the Temple Mount, and this was done without cracking a single piece of tile. The Jews got their temple, which was built over this ancient rock, and the daily sacrifice was resumed after untold centuries. The Jewish state was recognized, and the PLO was given statehood. Tourism in the entire area soared, and nations had to wait in line to make their commercial investments. It truly was a heady time. In the meantime, back in Rome where the Council of Regents was headquartered, things were also happening. The Beast, with little effort, encouraged the Council to create a new chairmanship and install him as the supreme leader. The Council's propaganda machine went into overdrive touting every achievement and promising the world that what was happening in the Middle East and Europe could happen globally. As a result, nations from around the globe gave up their sovereignty to the Council and most of their independence. The propaganda onslaught informed the world that the Council had voted to install their leader in the city of Jerusalem. Heads of state along with anyone else of any importance gathered in Jerusalem for the decision that would change the world. Everything was choreographed to maximize the accomplishments of the great Council and its great leader. When it came time for the Supreme Leader to speak, no one was disappointed. When he had finished, the collective body of leaders felt that they had worked together and achieved this tremendous success. And then he dropped a bombshell on his vast audience, which was broadcast around the world. His words were measured and carried with them the tone of a god. He informed the startled delegates that he was the product of a virgin birth himself. He claimed that his mother was impregnated by a great angel and the two of them bore this secret burden alone for all these years. He convinced the crowd that he knew at an early age that he was different and this certainly became evident to him in his early teenage years and early adulthood. In other words, he was given by the great angel "divine personhood." He went on to say that indeed it was true that when he was fighting for world peace, he was killed by a deranged man and his great "angel father" resurrected him from the dead. By this time the audience could take no more. They were gripped with emotions that could not be controlled as they wept and wailed over having been in the presence of this incredible person. Many were saying, "We knew he is different and has powers that no other man in history has demonstrated." They went on to cry, wail, and sob, saying things like "And just think we are here and have witnessed this history-making, world-changing event." It was almost more than they could take. The outnumbered medical staff was finally able to help those who had swooned and fainted recover to the point that the ceremony could continue. The Supreme Leader, otherwise known as the Beast, and his counsel entourage made their way inside the great Jewish temple, ending up in the Holy of Holies where the crowning chair awaited him. He was installed, or rather crowned, with a diadem that few people had ever imagined. The Holy of Holies was the most sacred part of the Jewish temple, and only the high priest could enter this holy place once a year, where he made sacrifice for his sins and the sins of the nation. This part of the ceremony was sent out by blazing cameras to every part of the world. The world now had itself a king and kingdom entailing one political system, one religion, and one legal organization. The tireless efforts of the Beast and his mantra had finally paid off. Anyone or any organization that opposed his absolute rule was considered traitor to the cause and was met with swift Council justice.

The first wrinkle in this utopia occurred when the council was slow in removing the outdoor constructions that made possible the world-changing installation of the supreme leader. For weeks the council back in Rome delayed and offered up petty excuses for not removing the structures in Jerusalem that made it impossible for the daily sacrifice to be restarted. They finally sent the word: "We regret that the Jewish temple and its altar cannot continue normal operations. In fact, our supreme leader has decided that the temple and its altar can never be opened because it has been deemed an obstruction to peace and progress." Outside of the Jewish community, no person or nation raised a hand in opposing this injustice. The world would soon learn that a coup had taken place and even common freedoms would never return. The stage is now set for the universal conflict of competing sovereignties between Satan and God.

The Beast

We are convinced that the angel that impregnated the Antichrist's mother was none other than Satan himself. Indeed, Satan had cloned himself into a human form that we refer to as the Beast. We are told here in chapter 13 that Satan gave the Beast his throne, power, and great authority. He is described as one who was like a leopard with features of a lion and bear. These terms are designed to remind us that this is a terrifying creature that will do anything to achieve his evil purposes. The Beast had seven heads and ten horns. We have already been told in chapter 12 that his father, Satan, had seven heads and ten horns, like father like son. The number *seven* in this case is a complete number representing complete maximum evil. He and his father were certainly totally evil and completely vile. The number *seven* could mean that he came from a line of kings of which he would be the last. But most likely it is referring to the seven hills that Rome sat upon and from which he carried on his massive evil operation. We are told this in chapter 17. The ten regents who served on the great Council that I proposed earlier are symbolized by the ten horns.

The Beast was then given authority to rule forty-two months or three-and-a-half years, which comprise the last three-and-a-half years of human history. He was given authority to rule the entire world with little or no interference. We are told it was granted to him to "make war with the saints and to overcome them and kill many." He had at his disposal all the power of the one world government, whereas the saints had only their testimony concerning the lordship of Jesus Christ and the promises of the Word of God. The Beast did not stand a chance of winning this battle.

The False Prophet

The first Beast came up out of the sea. The sea is a symbol of chaos, agitation, and turmoil. This is the stuff out of which the Beast rose to power. The False Prophet came up out of the earth, which suggests that he came to power in an orderly fashion through a worldwide organization. We know that this organization must have been the one world church. Through massive deception, these two partners in crime rose together and cooperated fully. It is no wonder that he is referred to as the "False Prophet." His only motive in life was to deceive and force the world to worship the Beast. Satan gave him extraordinary powers with which to deceive and manipulate the world's population. The claim used by the False Prophet was that their leader and lord had been killed and afterward raised from the dead. It would be very hard for leaders and common people to ignore this claim. I believe the claim was true. Satan resurrected his incarnated son in an effort to mimic the virgin birth of Christ and the resurrection of Jesus from the dead. We are told that the False Prophet had two horns like a lamb and spoke like a dragon. The two horns associated with a lamb denote gentleness, respect, and kindness. It was these traits that enabled the False Prophet to gain control over a worldwide religious system. But when he spoke, his true nature was revealed.

The Clone

In connection with the Beast and the False Prophet, an entity called "the Image" is disclosed to us. The question is whether this entity is a person or thing. It is my view that science finally did it. In the end times, the scientific community produced the perfect clone of the Beast. The one cloned was a master beast in every way. This clone was the exact image of the Antichrist. We are told in the book of Genesis that God said, "Let us make man in our image and in our likeness." The apostle Paul and the writer of the book of Hebrews declared that Jesus Christ is the exact image of the Father. We use that term pretty often when we refer to a child being in "the spitting image of his father." This creature, whatever we choose to call it, was very human down to the point of having to shave every morning. But he was also the perfect bionic man. Science had at last achieved its lifelong dream. The scientific goal was to produce a superhuman-like creature that had no conscience. He was like the False Prophet whose one mission in life was to force people to worship the

Beast and his father, Satan. I suspect that he was also used for lesser purposes like being a stand-in for the Beast in worldwide functions and to represent him when important mandates were delivered in person. My suggestion is that the clone spent much of his time in the Middle East making sure that all the mandates of the Council and its supreme leader were being carried out in detail.

A closer look at the mark of the Beast needs to be taken. We have already indicated that this mark might well be a secret name that the Beast will force his followers to receive on the forehead as a means of obedience and giving them access to trade. In reference to the popular end-time number *666*, the number *six* in Jewish thought represents the unredeemed man. This includes his potential. But for the most part the emphasis is on man's weakness, evil nature, and selfishness. If *six* represents all these things, when you raise it to the power of three, you have insight into the magnitude and nature of the Beast. Whatever the actual sign is going to be, it means that those who take it are doomed for the lake of fire where there is no release and no rest. It also means that for those who take it their total lives will be bound up with the Beast with no possibility of changing their convictions or reversing their choices.

The Revelation constantly reminds us that those whose names are not listed in the Book of Life are headed to the lake of fire (Rev 19:20) where their tragedy never ends. But those who take the mark of God are sealed and protected throughout all eternity. There is a sense in which every person on the planet in every generation is faced with this awesome choice. In our hearts, attitudes, and actions, we live out the Mark of God or the Mark of the Beast. This great reality demonstrated in the end times is a solemn warning to men and women in every generation.

Discussion Questions

1. We are told that the Dragon (Satan) stood on the shore of the sea and that the Beast came up out of the sea and the two were joined. Could this be the time when Satan incarnated himself into the Beast?

2. After this union between Satan and the Beast, descriptive words in verse 2 reveal the true nature of the Antichrist. Discuss.
3. When the Bible provides the information that the Beast encountered a fatal wound, is it saying that the Antichrist was killed and resurrected from the dead by Satan?
4. What was the role and function of the False Prophet in the book of Revelation?

REVELATION 14

The Fall of the Evil Empire

1 Then I looked, and behold, a Lamb standing on Mount Zion, and with Him one hundred *and* forty-four thousand, having His Father's name written on their foreheads. 2 And I heard a voice from heaven, like the voice of many waters, and like the voice of loud thunder. And I heard the sound of harpists playing their harps. 3 They sang as it were a new song before the throne, before the four living creatures, and the elders; and no one could learn that song except the hundred *and* forty-four thousand who were redeemed from the earth. 4 These are the ones who were not defiled with women, for they are virgins. These are the ones who follow the Lamb wherever He goes. These were redeemed from *among* men, *being* firstfruits to God and to the Lamb. 5 And in their mouth was found no deceit, for they are without fault before the throne of God.

6 Then I saw another angel flying in the midst of heaven, having the everlasting gospel to preach to those who dwell on the earth—to every nation, tribe, tongue, and people—7 saying with

a loud voice, "Fear God and give glory to Him, for the hour of His judgment has come; and worship Him who made heaven and earth, the sea and springs of water."

8And another angel followed, saying, "Babylon is fallen, is fallen, that great city, because she has made all nations drink of the wine of the wrath of her fornication."

9Then a third angel followed them, saying with a loud voice, "If anyone worships the beast and his image, and receives *his* mark on his forehead or on his hand, 10he himself shall also drink of the wine of the wrath of God, which is poured out full strength into the cup of His indignation. He shall be tormented with fire and brimstone in the presence of the holy angels and in the presence of the Lamb. 11And the smoke of their torment ascends forever and ever; and they have no rest day or night, who worship the beast and his image, and whoever receives the mark of his name."

12Here is the patience of the saints; here *are* those who keep the commandments of God and the faith of Jesus.

13Then I heard a voice from heaven saying to me, "Write: 'Blessed *are* the dead who die in the Lord from now on.'"

"Yes," says the Spirit, "that they may rest from their labors, and their works follow them."

14Then I looked, and behold, a white cloud, and on the cloud sat *One* like the Son of Man, having on His head a golden crown, and in His hand a sharp sickle. 15And another angel came out of the temple, crying with a loud voice to Him who sat on the cloud, "Thrust in Your sickle and reap, for the time has come for You to reap, for the harvest of the earth is ripe." 16So He who sat on the cloud thrust in His sickle on the earth, and the earth was reaped.

17Then another angel came out of the temple which is in heaven, he also having a sharp sickle. 18And another angel came out from the altar, who had power over fire, and he cried with a loud cry to him who had the sharp sickle, saying, "Thrust in your sharp sickle and gather the clusters of the vine of the earth, for her grapes are fully ripe." 19So the angel thrust his sickle into the earth and gathered the vine of the earth, and threw *it* into the great winepress of the wrath of God. 20And the winepress was trampled outside the city, and blood came out of the winepress, up to the horses' bridles, for one thousand six hundred furlongs.

The Lamb and the Saints

In chapter 14, we meet the Lamb and 144,000 saints who were selected and chosen for a special work during the millennial reign of Christ. We have met this group before and will meet them again at the start of the one-thousand-year reign of Christ. We met them in chapter 6 when the Lamb opened the fifth seal. This was a small nucleus of saints found under the golden altar in heaven. They were given white robes and told to wait a little longer until their total number could be completed or reached. It is very important to note that these saints were found under the golden altar in heaven. The altar is a place of sacrifice, and these saints had given their all in violent deaths. We saw the completed group in chapter 7 when they were selected and sealed with the Mark of God. Now we meet them in heaven on Mount Zion, standing with the Lamb Who also had given

His life in a violent death. They along with the Lamb led heaven in one of the greatest worship services that glorious place would ever experience.

The Three Chosen Angels

No one will ever be able to say that God did not employ all His vast resources in order to bring people to Himself and give light to the human race. In this case He employed three mighty angels. The first angel preached the gospel to the entire world at a time when the grace and mercy of God was about to run out. Even at the end of human history, God was still appealing to sinners. Not a stone was left unturned; not an area was left without hearing the gospel. The message had to do with repentance, turning to God, and worshiping the Lord of the universe. The second angel cried out that Babylon had fallen. Babylon was that wicked system contrived and forced onto the world by Satan, the Beast, and his image. This second angel was trying to head off that portion of the world's population who had not yet taken the Mark of the Beast. When hearing the demands of the gospel, many people would be inclined to say, "We already worship a messiah and a god who has proven himself by providing peace, prosperity, and much progress. He has brought good news to our world, so why should we choose one that we have not seen and one who has not already provided these great benefits for our families and friends?" The second angel was declaring to this group who had not taken the mark of the Beast that "This wicked system and its leader cannot help you. Don't take a chance; don't take the risk, because this wicked system that the Beast rules over is already in the process of collapse." In fact, the angel declared that Babylon had already fallen within.

The third angel came on the scene to warn this group that if they took the Mark of the Beast and continued on their present course, they would end up in the Lake of Fire (Hell). Words to describe the final destination of the wicked dead and those who bear the Mark of the Beast are inadequate. There is no language to describe the destiny of the wicked. Is this destination a massive furnace that contains a temperature that we cannot calculate? Whatever our conclusions about the Lake of Fire (Hell) and the destiny of the wicked, the most important thing about it is that all who arrive at that place will be finally and completely separated from God and all that is good. It also means that the wicked will have to endure each other throughout all eternity. They will also be forced to face every lost opportunity squandered and every remembrance of what might have been had they listened to their family members, friends, and everything that the gospel had promised. Those prospects will be more terrible and terrifying than anything we know about Hell at this present time.

The Reaping of the Church

The apostle John was told that only the bliss of heaven awaited the saints or believers who died from here on out. The door of heaven sprang open, and the mighty Messiah King was seen coming on a cloud with a sharp sickle in his hand. It is concluded that the time to reap the whole earth had arrived and the Lord Jesus Christ reaped the entire earth of the saints of God, both the living and the dead. What was happening here is nothing less than the great general resurrection of all believers. It is this same event that is described in more graphic terms by the apostle Paul in 1 Thessalonians 4:14–17.

This is the glorious resurrection day for which we all have waited and yearned. I must confess that I am a little bit disappointed that the Revelation account doesn't have more hype in it and more sensationalism. At the very least, I feel some of the elements of Paul's more graphic account (1 Thessalonians 4:14–17) of this same event could have been included. Everything sounds so mundane and matter-of-fact and kind of earthy. The truth of the matter is that any discussion or reference to the resurrection of the saints should include all the descriptions that are found in the Bible. For our purposes and further clarity, you need to read and consider the following references from Jesus in Mark 13:26–27, Paul in 1 Corinthians 15 and 1 Thessalonians 4:14–17, and the apostle John in Revelation 1:7.

But this is the way God wanted it to be. His ways are not our ways, and His emotional needs are not ours. In fact, Jesus favored the concept of reaping and often used it to describe this great event. But there are some things we do know. We know, for example, from other places in Scripture that a team of mighty angels will be used in this reaping because our Lord says so. We know that the great trumpet will be sounded because the Bible tells us so. We know that every eye on planet earth will see Him at His coming because the Word teaches this great truth. God's ways are not man's ways, and had we needed more information, God would have provided it. Note that this great and glorious resurrection day for the saints will occur just before the seven bowls of the wrath of God are poured out on earth. This means that the church will be on planet earth during the opening of the Seals and the sounding of the Trumpets. I continue to ask myself if the church as we know it today is ready for this kind of end-time living. I also wonder if we pastors and lay leaders are fully aware of our responsibility to get His church ready for whatever it encounters in the end-time period.

The Reaping of the Wicked

There are two reapings discussed in Revelation 14. We have already addressed the first reaping, the rapture of the church, that occurs in verses 14–16. In verses 17–20 we find a second reaping, which is the reaping of the wicked.

There are three things that should be said about this reaping. First, this reaping was by the risen Christ. Even though an angel said the words, the command was given by the Messiah.

Second, this reaping was partial. We know this is true because the great majority of the wicked were on earth during the last three-and-a-half years of human history and went through the throes of the wrath of God.

Third, this reaping was achieved by great violence. We are told that when it occurred blood flowed out of the winepress rising as high as the horse's bridles (around four feet) for a distance of about two hundred miles.

It is conceivable that an event like this could literally take place. There are wet weather streambeds in the Middle East that run deep with water during the spring rains, while the rest of the year they lie dormant. Am I insisting that we give this event a literal interpretation? The answer is no. What we have here is a figure of speech called oriental exaggeration, which is a legitimate communication tool in apocalyptic literature. The angel was saying to John that this event would be extremely violent.

Scenario 2
The Resurrection Day

I need to say a few words about the great and glorious resurrection day and God's plan for His people, which includes the reaping (rapture) of the church. First of all, the term *rapture* is neither mentioned in the Revelation nor in the New Testament itself with regard to the church. In Jesus's language the term *reaping* is more appropriate and scriptural. But the question I want us to grapple with is, What is going to happen on our personal resurrection day? Without going into a lot of background, I want to share with our readers a conclusion that I have reluctantly come to. When true believers die on earth and their bodies are laid to rest in the grave somewhere, those true believers go directly to heaven and at the point of arrival are given heavenly bodies. Over and over in the activities of heaven, we see the saints of God involved in the kind of activities that require bodies. For example, we see the saints playing harps, singing loudly, and offering up untold praises to God. In addition, we see them carrying palm branches, and all of them are wearing white robes or clothes that are appropriate for heaven. Taking a clue from Jesus concerning His resurrection and glorified body, my response is that those activities require that they be in possession of their heavenly bodies. Jesus's pre-resurrection body died on the cruel cross of Calvary. The Holy Spirit is emphatic that Jesus really died on the cross and the body that Joseph of Arimathea put in that tomb was really a dead human body. By the third day, it would have been experiencing rigor mortis and the odor of death. But when Jesus was raised up from the dead by the Father, it is my view His pre-resurrection body was incorporated into His glorified body. This truth is demonstrated by His resurrection body. He was recognized when He stood before His disciples. And He Himself said, "Come touch Me, and place your fingers into My scars in My hands, feet, and side. In fact, bring Me something to eat so I can demonstrate to you that I'm not just a spirit, but I am your risen Lord" (Luke 24:39.) In answer to the question of what is going to happen on resurrection day, Paul in the book of Thessalonians made a remarkable statement. He said concerning those saints and family members who had died on earth, "God will bring with Him those who have fallen asleep in Jesus" (1 Thessalonians 4:17), on resurrection day. But the question is, What will happen on resurrection day when we appear before our earthly graves? It is my conviction that God wants to leave with this pagan world a definitive answer in the form of an open and empty tomb. On resurrection morning, those who are dead will come back to their graves for the purpose of leaving that grave open and empty for the whole world to see and to speak the final word about death. Our graves will be opened, not by us but by our Lord, and our earthly bodies will be subsumed and incorporated into our resurrection bodies as was the case with Jesus. I do not understand all this, but I am informed by the Word, which does understand and has the power to make it happen. The saints of God will leave a lasting word for the entire universe, namely, "My old tomb is empty with the exception of my grave clothes, and death is already defeated." Finally then, the words of the apostle Paul can be fulfilled when he said, "Death is swallowed up in victory" (1 Corinthians 15:52).

Discussion Questions

1. What does the group found standing with the Lamb on Mount Zion in heaven have in common with Him?
2. Why do you think God employed three angels at the beginning of the great tribulation period?
3. We are faced in this chapter with the second coming of Christ and the rapture of the church (verse 14–16). Do these two events happen simultaneously?

4. Jesus did not use the term *rapture* to indicate His second coming. Instead, He used the term *reaping*. Why do you think some people still insist that the rapture/reaping takes place in chapter 4?

REVELATION 15

The End of Mercy and Grace

1Then I saw another sign in heaven, great and marvelous: seven angels having the seven last plagues, for in them the wrath of God is complete.

2And I saw *something* like a sea of glass mingled with fire, and those who have the victory over the beast, over his image and over his mark *and* over the number of his name, standing on the sea of glass, having harps of God. 3They sing the song of Moses, the servant of God, and the song of the Lamb, saying: "Great and marvelous *are* our works, Lord God Almighty! Just and true *are* Your ways, O King of the saints! 4Who shall not fear You, O Lord, and glorify Your name? For *You* alone *are* holy. For all nations shall come and worship before You, For Your judgments have been manifested."

5After these things I looked, and behold, the temple of the tabernacle of the testimony in heaven was opened. 6And out of the temple came the seven angels having the seven plagues, clothed in pure bright linen, and having their chests girded with golden bands. 7Then one of

> the four living creatures gave to the seven angels seven golden bowls full of the wrath of God who lives forever and ever. 8The temple was filled with smoke from the glory of God and from His power, and no one was able to enter the temple till the seven plagues of the seven angels were completed.

This chapter is designed to get us ready for what is about to happen in human history. We are told that what is about to happen is a great sign. Something has to be extremely important to rise to the level of a sign, which in Greek is called *simaion* [sigh-May-on]. The last time we met a sign, in fact two signs, was in chapter 12 where we were presented with an austere, majestic woman about to give birth to a male child. A fiery Red Dragon was positioned before her to devour her child as soon as it was born.

It seems to me that the announcement of this third sign—which could mean a wonder, miracle, or window into divine reality—brought about a state of shock for both men and angels. The sign tells us that the last three-and-a-half years of earth's history was about to begin. It also tells us that the instruments that would be used during this last three-and-a-half years of human history would be seven plagues saturated with the wrath of God. God intends for us to make the connection between these plagues and the plagues of Egypt that demonstrated His victory over the false gods of Egypt and its Pharaoh. The seven last plagues would be symbolized by the use of seven bowls. Men and angels entered a state of shock because no one had ever heard of the wrath of God being poured out undiluted in full strength upon earth. No one had ever seen this side of God in action in which mercy and grace had come to an end. No one knew what it might look like and what forms it might take, and so there was joy mixed with dread.

A new group of saints is pictured standing on the sea of glass, worshiping and praising the Creator God and the Lamb. They probably had freshly arrived from the battlefield and met violent deaths because they would not receive the Mark of the Beast. They would not give up their faith and commitment to Christ, and they refused to deny the Word of God. Instead, they wore the Mark of God on their foreheads. They knew that their vindication was soon to arrive and that total victory was on the way. These awesome saints had the Mark of God written all over their lives. Their convictions and complete trust were in the Word of God. The sea of glass in this case symbolizes complete security, safety, and the complete absence of any chaos and turmoil. This last dreadful reality had its beginning when the Beast was crowned king in the Holy of Holies in the great temple at Jerusalem. It would end when the world witnessed this ruined and destroyed planet. The Old Testament prophets, Paul, and Jesus Himself (Matthew 24:15) referred to this event as the Abomination of Desolation. This transitional chapter is about to usher us into the greatest tragedy men and angels have ever witnessed.

Discussion Questions

1. There are three signs mentioned in the book of Revelation. One of these is mentioned in this chapter. A sign represents a unique window of truth made available to the believer. Why do you think the term *sign* was used in this chapter?
2. What is another word in this chapter that means the same thing as *plague*?
3. Verse 2 mentions that John also saw "those who had won the victory from the Beast." According to our guide, who were these people?

REVELATION 16

The Undiluted Wrath of God

1 Then I heard a loud voice from the temple saying to the seven angels, "Go and pour out the bowls of the wrath of God on the earth."

2 So the first went and poured out his bowl upon the earth, and a foul and loathsome sore came upon the men who had the mark of the beast and those who worshiped his image.

3 Then the second angel poured out his bowl on the sea, and it became blood as of a dead *man;* and every living creature in the sea died.

4 Then the third angel poured out his bowl on the rivers and springs of water, and they became blood. 5 And I heard the angel of the waters saying: "You are righteous, O Lord, The One who is and who was and who is to be, Because You have judged these things. 6 For they have shed the blood of saints and prophets, And You have given them blood to drink. For it is their just due."

7And I heard another from the altar saying, "Even so, Lord God Almighty, true and righteous *are* Your judgments."

8Then the fourth angel poured out his bowl on the sun, and power was given to him to scorch men with fire. 9And men were scorched with great heat, and they blasphemed the name of God who has power over these plagues; and they did not repent and give Him glory.

10Then the fifth angel poured out his bowl on the throne of the beast, and his kingdom became full of darkness; and they gnawed their tongues because of the pain. 11They blasphemed the God of heaven because of their pains and their sores, and did not repent of their deeds.

12Then the sixth angel poured out his bowl on the great river Euphrates, and its water was dried up, so that the way of the kings from the east might be prepared. 13And I saw three unclean spirits like frogs *coming* out of the mouth of the dragon, out of the mouth of the beast, and out of the mouth of the false prophet. 14For they are spirits of demons, performing signs, *which* go out to the kings of the earth and of the whole world, to gather them to the battle of that great day of God Almighty.
15"Behold, I am coming as a thief. Blessed *is* he who watches, and keeps his garments, lest he walk naked and they see his shame."
16And they gathered them together to the place called in Hebrew, Armageddon.

17Then the seventh angel poured out his bowl into the air, and a loud voice came out of the temple of heaven, from the throne, saying, "It is done!" 18And there were noises and thunderings and lightnings; and there was a great earthquake, such a mighty and great earthquake as had not occurred since men were on the earth. 19Now the great city was divided into three parts, and the cities of the nations fell. And great Babylon was remembered before God, to give her the cup of the wine of the fierceness of His wrath. 20Then every island fled away, and the mountains were not found. 21And great hail from heaven fell upon men, *each hailstone* about the weight of a talent. Men blasphemed God because of the plague of the hail, since that plague was exceedingly great.

The seven special angels were given seven golden bowls full of the wrath of God and were told to commence their work. Remember, in the Seal judgment, one-fourth of the human population and the physical earth were destroyed. In the Trumpet judgment, the destruction factor was increased to one-third. Now in this last judgment, the destruction level would be 100 percent, representing roughly four billion people.

The first bowl was poured out on unbelieving humanity who bore the Mark of the Beast. The bodies of those who had rejected the gospel were soon totally enveloped with a disease of open sores that carried with it pain that could not be described. We are told that the only relief they could get was by gritting their teeth and cursing God. Probably the sores resembled a blood disease that we used to call carbuncles. A more common name is a horribly painful infectious skin boil, caused by the bacteria *Staphylococcus aureus*. In these last days, all earth dwellers were singled out, and the retribution level was almost 100 percent.

The second bowl was poured out on the oceans and seas, and the entire oceanic water system was turned to blood. In just a few days, the stench alone would be impossible to bear and a vital food source completely removed. Common sense leads us to believe that the effect of these bowls should be taken literally.

The third angel poured out his bowl on all freshwater supply. These waters were turned into blood also. Only those who had stored up a little freshwater would be able to survive for a while.

The fourth bowl was poured out on the sun, which would have brought havoc to all the celestial bodies. The atmosphere of the earth had now been removed, and this beautiful star we call the sun had been given additional nuclear energy by the fourth angel. Many were scorched to death, and those who survived probably experienced third-degree burns. Nothing like this had ever happened in our universe as far as we know. It is no wonder that men and angels went into shock when it was announced that the wrath of God was about to be poured out on humanity.

The fifth angel poured out his bowl on the throne of the Beast. Along with the previous terrifying judgments and retributions came darkness that had no equal. We know that darkness overwhelmed the Egyptians and its Pharaoh, but this darkness before us now was physically and emotionally unbearable. We are not told how long it lasted. It could have lasted over an extended period of time. It would be as if the remaining population left on planet earth had suddenly gone blind, totally blind. With their bodies gripped with terrifying pain and their world completely shut down by darkness, the only thing left was to curse and gnash their teeth and of course blame and curse God and the saints. It is safe to say that most, if not all, of these people under this level of pain and suffering wanted to die or wanted to commit suicide but could not. In God's wisdom He allowed the Beast and the False Prophet to escape from their headquarters in Rome to do one of their final things.

The sixth bowl was poured out on the river Euphrates, which is a landmark of division between north and south in the Middle East. The great river was dried up, making a way for a massive army located in the north to march on Palestine and the region of

Jerusalem. Evidently, this mercenary army had been held in reserve and protected from the death and destruction of the wrath poured out from the other bowls. The Beast and the False Prophet rushed to this area, and with their massive amounts of stolen cash, they enlisted this army to dethrone God and His Messiah. This army, which could not be numbered, made their way to the hill of Megiddo in Northern Israel, which would become their campaign headquarters. We are held in suspense about the outcome of this looming conflict until we get to chapter 19. It is worthy to note that this trinity of evil (Satan, the Beast, and the False Prophet) was gathered to persuade this vast army to take part in this "mother of all wars." Satan was there along with the Beast and False Prophet. Everything that Satan, his partners, and his incarnated son did in these last days was counterfeit. The gathering of this trinity of evil—the Beast, the False Prophet, and Satan (Revelation 16:13)—at the Euphrates River was an effort to compete with and dethrone God. The Beast threw down the gauntlet to the Messiah of God and challenged Him to meet him in one last great battle in which "winner takes all" would be the reward. I can believe that the Beast promised this army all the booty they could ever want as a bonus.

The seventh and last bowl was poured out in the air. Heaven and earth were both brought to their knees by this last judgment that culminated in the greatest earthquake the world had ever witnessed. One-hundred-pound hailstones fell from the sky. Apparently all standing buildings around the entire world were brought down, and Jerusalem was divided into three parts. Some Old Testament prophets told about an altered Jerusalem in the end times that includes a vast cleavage through the Mount of Olives that would accommodate a river that will run from the Mediterranean Sea to the Dead Sea (Zechariah 14:1–15).

Discussion Questions

1. We see seals broken in chapter 6, trumpets blasted in chapters 8 and 9, and now bowls poured out in this chapter. In just a few words for the sake of review, what was the

general, basic result of each broken seal, trumpet blast, and bowl poured out? Do not describe the result of each seal, trumpet blast, or bowl; but discuss the overall impact of the seals, trumpets, and bowls. Be general, not specific.
2. Upon whom were the contents of the seals, trumpets, and bowls poured out?
3. How did they respond? (See verses 9, 11, 14, 16, and 21.)

REVELATION 17

The Power and Personalities Operating behind the Scenes

1 Then one of the seven angels who had the seven bowls came and talked with me, saying to me, "Come, I will show you the judgment of the great harlot who sits on many waters, 2 with whom the kings of the earth committed fornication, and the inhabitants of the earth were made drunk with the wine of her fornication."

3 So he carried me away in the Spirit into the wilderness. And I saw a woman sitting on a scarlet beast *which was* full of names of blasphemy, having seven heads and ten horns. 4 The woman was arrayed in purple and scarlet, and adorned with gold and precious stones and pearls, having in her hand a golden cup full of abominations and the filthiness of her fornication. 5 And on her forehead a name *was* written: MYSTERY, BABYLON THE GREAT, THE MOTHER OF HARLOTS AND OF THE ABOMINATIONS OF THE EARTH.

6 I saw the woman, drunk with the blood of the saints and with the blood of the martyrs of

Jesus. And when I saw her, I marveled with great amazement.

7But the angel said to me, "Why did you marvel? I will tell you the mystery of the woman and of the beast that carries her, which has the seven heads and the ten horns. 8The beast that you saw was, and is not, and will ascend out of the bottomless pit and go to perdition. And those who dwell on the earth will marvel, whose names are not written in the Book of Life from the foundation of the world, when they see the beast that was, and is not, and yet is.

9"Here *is* the mind which has wisdom: The seven heads are seven mountains on which the woman sits. 10There are also seven kings. Five have fallen, one is, *and* the other has not yet come. And when he comes, he must continue a short time. 11The beast that was, and is not, is himself also the eighth, and is of the seven, and is going to perdition.

12"The ten horns which you saw are ten kings who have received no kingdom as yet, but they receive authority for of ne hour as kings with the beast. 13These are of one mind, and they will give their power and authority to the beast. 14These will make war with the Lamb, and the Lamb will overcome them, for He is Lord of lords and King of kings; and those *who are* with Him *are* called, chosen, and faithful."

15Then he said to me, "The waters which you saw, where the harlot sits, are peoples, multitudes, nations, and tongues. 16And the ten horns which you saw on the beast, these will hate the harlot, make her desolate and naked, eat her flesh and burn her with fire. 17For God has put it into

> their hearts to fulfill His purpose, to be of one mind, and to give their kingdom to the beast, until the words of God are fulfilled. 18And the woman whom you saw is that great city which reigns over the kings of the earth."

Chapters 17 and 18 serve as a literary device called an interlude designed to pause the fever-pitched action in order to define and identify the personalities and dynamics operating behind the scenes. There comes a time when we need to stop, reflect, and consider who the personalities and power brokers are behind the takeover of the world.

One of the seven angels came to the apostle John and offered to show and interpret for him the key personalities. The angel carried John away from the violence and noise, and he was shocked over what he saw. A gaudy woman was riding on the back of a creature that looked something like a mammoth spider with a red body. The woman was identified as the Great Harlot. She sat on many waters and Seven Hills. The many waters represent masses of people, and the seven hills identify her residence as that of Rome in Europe. Her clothing and accessories displayed her as a very wealthy woman who was more than glad to show off this wealth. She had many tattoos, and on her forehead and body were the inscriptions "Babylon the Great," the mother of harlots. It appears that she had two main vocations. The first was a vocation of seduction. As a result, she seduced every person and everything that came within her reach, especially the great men and women of the world. The purpose of this seduction was designed to convince these great people that they should surrender their sovereignty and independence to the Beast along with the countries they represented. Her second vocation was that of killing the saints and creating martyrs. After all, the saints of God had been declared traitors to the beast's one world nation. They were deemed a threat to peace, prosperity, and progress. She and her henchmen tracked down these believers and killed them. This is expressed in the statement, "She was intoxicated with the blood of the saints" (Revelation 17:6). It appears that this woman was a mistress of the

Beast upon which she rode. The fact that he had been raised from the dead by his father, Satan, did not hurt his cause at all. He had seven heads, which symbolized the Seven Hills where Rome was located. It also tells us that he came from a long line of ruthless dictators whose goal was to take over the entire world. One of his heads bore the mark of death, symbolizing a pseudo-resurrection. Because of this, the entire world believed that he was a man of God and could be trusted. The ten horns that he wore were described as ten kings who had no kingdoms. It is my view that these ten men made up the most powerful organization on the planet, which I choose to call the Council of Regents whose headquarters was in Rome. Their one purpose for existing was to assist the Beast in taking over the world and maintaining his control. The mighty angel reminded John that this creature, which was Satan incarnate, came from the bottomless pit and would one day find himself thrown into the Lake of Fire. But one thing the Beast and his cronies did not anticipate was a sudden interruption from heaven. We know that from the fifth bowl the wrath of God was poured out on the Beast's throne and the collapse and destruction sent him running for his life along with his sidekick, the False Prophet. Our storyline will continue soon, and we will see how the Beast and the False Prophet fared. This interlude has shown us who the real culprits are as well as a great deal about their nature.

Discussion Questions

1. What does the writer of this study guide believe the purpose of this chapter in the Revelation is?
2. Who did John identify as the woman riding the Beast?
3. What would happen to her eventually (verse 16)?
4. Who is the Beast? Check the first seven lines of the first scenario in chapter 13 to review.

REVELATION 18

The Cost of Surrendering to Evil

1After these things I saw another angel coming down from heaven, having great authority, and the earth was illuminated with his glory. 2And he cried mightily with a loud voice, saying, "Babylon the great is fallen, is fallen, and has become a dwelling place of demons, a prison for every foul spirit, and a cage for every unclean and hated bird! 3For all the nations have drunk of the wine of the wrath of her fornication, the kings of the earth have committed fornication with her, and the merchants of the earth have become rich through the abundance of her luxury."

4And I heard another voice from heaven saying, "Come out of her, my people, lest you share in her sins, and lest you receive of her plagues. 5For her sins have reached to heaven, and God has remembered her iniquities. 6Render to her just as she rendered to you, and repay her double according to her works; in the cup which she has mixed, mix double for her. 7In the measure that she glorified herself and lived luxuriously, in the same measure give her torment and sorrow; for she says in her heart, 'I sit *as* queen, and am no widow, and will not see sorrow.' 8Therefore her plagues will come in one day—death and mourning and famine. And she will be utterly burned with fire, for strong *is* the Lord God who judges her.

9"The kings of the earth who committed fornication and lived luxuriously with her will weep and lament for her, when they see the smoke of her burning, 10standing at a distance for fear of her torment, saying, 'Alas, alas, that great city Babylon, that mighty city! For in one hour your judgment has come.'

11"And the merchants of the earth will weep and mourn over her, for no one buys their merchandise anymore: 12merchandise of gold and silver, precious stones and pearls, fine linen and purple, silk and scarlet, every kind of citron wood, every kind of object of ivory, every kind of object of most precious wood, bronze, iron, and marble; 13and cinnamon and incense, fragrant oil and frankincense, wine and oil, fine flour and wheat, cattle and sheep, horses and chariots, and bodies and souls of men. 14The fruit that your soul longed for has gone from you, and all the things which are rich and splendid have gone from you, and you shall find them no more at all. 15The merchants of these things, who became rich by her, will stand at a distance for fear of her torment, weeping and wailing, 16and saying, 'Alas, alas, that great city that was clothed in fine linen, purple, and scarlet, and adorned with gold and precious stones and pearls! 17For in one hour such great riches came to nothing.' Every shipmaster, all who travel by ship, sailors, and as many as trade on the sea, stood at a distance

18and cried out when they saw the smoke of her burning, saying, 'What *is* like this great city?'

19"They threw dust on their heads and cried out, weeping and wailing, and saying, 'Alas, alas, that great city, in which all who had ships on the sea became rich by her wealth! For in one hour she is made desolate.'

20"Rejoice over her, O heaven, and *you* holy apostles and prophets, for God has avenged you on her!"

21Then a mighty angel took up a stone like a great millstone and threw *it* into the sea, saying, "Thus with violence the great city Babylon shall be thrown down, and shall not be found anymore. 22The sound of harpists, musicians, flutists, and trumpeters shall not be heard in you anymore. No craftsman of any craft shall be found in you anymore, and the sound of a millstone shall not be heard in you anymore. 23The light of a lamp shall not shine in you anymore, and the voice of bridegroom and bride shall not be heard in you anymore. For your merchants were the great men of the earth, for by your sorcery all the nations were deceived. 24And in her was found the blood of prophets and saints, and of all who were slain on the earth."

If chapter 17 shows us the personalities and power brokers working behind the scenes, then chapter 18 shows us the results and cost to the human race when it surrendered themselves and their institutions to evil. Babylon the Great is another name given to the woman. As the narrative continues, we find out that we were not talking about a woman per se in chapter 17 but rather of the vastly enlarged and magnificent city of Rome, or perhaps Europe. But it goes beyond that. In the final analysis, we are talking about a system that was taken over and refined to its highest level by the Beast and his cohorts. In the last days, Rome will be the place to go to and the city of all cities. Nowadays people want to go to Paris, some to Las Vegas, and some to the great city of New York. But in the end times, Rome will be the place to go. Its beauty and splendor will be published and extolled in every medium on the planet. But after the fifth bowl of wrath is poured out, the collapse and carnage will be indescribable. The only ones who will be willing to inhabit these ruins are demons, foul spirits, and hated birds. Hated birds in this case probably represent nocturnal birds that are deemed to be linked to the underworld and therefore would never be used as pets. A few lines in chapter 18 adequately describe the final state of the Great Harlot, i.e., Babylon the Great, and the system over which a maniacal Antichrist ruled.

> So will Babylon, the great city, be thrown down with violence, and will not be found any longer. And the sound of harpists and musicians and flute players and trumpeters will not be heard in you any longer; and no craftsman of any craft will be found in you any longer; and the sound of a mill will not be heard in you any longer; and the light of a lamp will not shine in you any longer; and the voice of the bridegroom and bride will not be heard in you any longer. (Revelation 18:22–23)

> The saddest words from tongue or pen are the words "what might have been." (Greenleaf)

Discussion Questions

1. According to the study guide, what is the relationship of this chapter to chapter 17?
2. The guide suggests the woman in this chapter was not a real person but a city. Why do you think God chose to identify the city of Rome with this woman?
3. Discuss "the system" the guide refers to in this chapter.

A BRIEF STUDY GUIDE FOR THE BOOK OF REVELATION

4. Thinking out loud: If John were writing Revelation today, what city do you think he would use? Would he keep Rome or choose another?

REVELATION 19

Quantum Worship

1After these things I heard a loud voice of a great multitude in heaven, saying, "Alleluia! Salvation and glory and honor and power *belong* to the Lord our God! 2For true and righteous *are* His judgments, because He has judged the great harlot who corrupted the earth with her fornication; and He has avenged on her the blood of His servants *shed* by her." 3Again they said, "Alleluia! Her smoke rises up forever and ever!" 4And the twenty-four elders and the four living creatures fell down and worshiped God who sat on the throne, saying, "Amen! Alleluia!" 5Then a voice came from the throne, saying, "Praise our God, all you His servants and those who fear Him, both small and great!"

6And I heard, as it were, the voice of a great multitude, as the sound of many waters and as the sound of mighty thunderings, saying, "Alleluia! For the Lord God Omnipotent reigns! 7Let us be glad and rejoice and give Him glory, for the marriage of the Lamb has come, and His wife has made herself ready." 8And to her it was granted to be arrayed in fine linen, clean and bright, for the fine linen is the righteous acts of the saints.

9Then he said to me, "Write: 'Blessed *are* those who are called to the marriage supper of the Lamb!'" And he said to me, "These are the true sayings of God." 10And I fell at his feet to worship him. But he said to me, "See *that you do* not *do that!* I am your fellow servant, and of your brethren who have the testimony of Jesus. Worship God! For the testimony of Jesus is the spirit of prophecy."

11Now I saw heaven opened, and behold, a white horse. And He who sat on him *was* called Faithful and True, and in righteousness He judges and makes war. 12His eyes *were* like a flame of fire, and on His head *were* many crowns. He had a name written that no one knew except Himself. 13He *was* clothed with a robe dipped in blood, and His name is called The Word of God. 14And the armies in heaven, clothed in fine linen, white and clean, followed Him on white horses. 15Now out of His mouth goes a sharp sword, that with it He should strike the nations. And He Himself will rule them with a rod of iron. He Himself treads the winepress of the fierceness and wrath of Almighty God. 16And He has on *His* robe and on His thigh a name written: KING OF KINGS AND LORD OF LORDS.

17Then I saw an angel standing in the sun; and he cried with a loud voice, saying to all the birds that fly in the midst of heaven, "Come and gather together for the supper of the great God, 18that you may eat the flesh of kings, the flesh of captains, the flesh of mighty men, the flesh of horses and of those who sit on them, and the flesh of all *people,* free and slave, both small and great."

19And I saw the beast, the kings of the earth, and their armies, gathered together to make war against Him who sat on the horse and against His army. 20Then the beast was captured, and with him the false prophet who worked signs in his presence, by which he deceived those who received the mark of the beast and those who worshiped his image. These two were cast alive into the lake of fire burning with brimstone. 21And the rest were killed with the sword which proceeded from the mouth of Him who sat on the horse. And all the birds were filled with their flesh.

The Four Hallelujahs

The mood is changed completely, and the tone is one of great joy and victory. In the early verses, we encounter worship at its best, some of which was captured in Handel's great "Messiah." What we have here is quantum worship. The church had been raptured or reaped (Jesus's favorite term) in chapter 14. Satan's throne had been destroyed and plunged into eternal darkness in chapter 13. The seven Bowls of the Wrath of God had been poured out on a wicked and rebellious humanity in chapter 16. Finally, God and His people had been vindicated.

The Judgment Seat of Christ

Now, in this chapter, between verses 6 and 7, we encounter the judgment seat, or the bema, of Christ. The apostle Paul made mention of this event three times in the New Testament (Romans 14:10–12; 1 Corinthians 3:10–15; 2 Corinthians 5:10). It seems to be clear that the purpose of the judgment seat of Christ is not to determine whether a person is saved or not but how they have handled the accountability issue. At the Judgment Seat of Christ, our Lord will require that we explain all our choices, priorities, and values and certainly our worldview since trusting Him. He will listen to us as we explain what we have done with all the opportunities that our risen Lord has given us. At the top of this list will be how we used opportunities to bring people to Christ and heaven.

So we are told that this judgment event with Christ for all believers will take place. We are also given some clues about what this event will settle. The one thing that is lacking is when it will occur. In the book of Revelation (19:7–9), the reader will encounter the wonderful event of the wedding of the Lamb and His bride, the church. Immediately a great angel instructed John to write down what he was about to say. "Blessed are those who are invited to the wedding supper of the Lamb" (Revelation 19:9). Special emphasis should be placed on the word *invited*. If this invitation belonged to every believer who went to heaven, then there would be no purpose for the angel to repeat it. But this invitation to the great wedding banquet of the Lamb and His bride is not automatically available to every believer according to the angel's announcement. This invitation as given suggests that the believer must qualify to attend this great reception of honor. This tells me that the time when believers will appear before the judgment seat of Christ is just prior to the wedding of the Lamb and His bride found in this chapter 19 of Revelation. Obviously, some believers will not qualify to attend this banquet of all banquets. The apostle Paul offered the same suggestion in 1 Corinthians 3:10–15. It is my belief that believers will (or will not) receive their crowns at this judgment event. The purpose of the crowns that are provided will be for us to lay them at the feet of Jesus at the imminent marriage banquet. Can you imagine a believer being at the marriage banquet with no crown to offer the King? The judgment seat of Christ will also settle the leadership role of believers for all eternity. The apostle Paul and Jesus Himself clearly indicated there will be some kind of divine gradation among believers in the eternal state.

LEONARD QUICK, M. DIV.

The Wedding and the Marriage Supper of the Lamb

The long-awaited event of both Christ and His church had finally come. Before us is what we call the marriage of the Lamb. His bride, dressed out in pure white, was none other than the church. The bride and the saints wore white, which represents the righteousness, holiness, and purity of the Lamb and the righteous acts of the saints. It was an awesome spectacle that would never lose its effect on history or eternity. Following the wedding was a banquet, or as some translations say the marriage supper of the Lamb. Nothing was spared in this supper or reception. Who knows, we might be served ten courses of manna, and each course will perfectly fill and satisfy our palates.

The Third Coming of Christ

The final scene in this triumphant chapter presents to us the victorious Messiah riding on a white stallion. In the Roman military, the victorious Caesar with his troops paraded their captives through the streets of Rome. In this scene, the Messiah King and His troops paraded from heaven to earth in great splendor and victory. In this return, He touched down in Jerusalem on the Mount of Olives along with His saints. The purpose of this third coming is to counter the challenge laid down by the Beast to meet Him on the battlefield at Armageddon. This is supposed to be the mother of all battles.

Another purpose of this third coming is to set up the Messiah King's throne in Jerusalem and prepare for the millennial kingdom, which was about to begin. He and His army had returned to take up the challenge that was posed by the Beast and False Prophet. The mother of all battles turned out to be no battle at all. The Beast and the False Prophet were immediately seized and cast into the lake of fire. Our Lord Jesus spoke one or two words, and this vast army of the enemy lay dead across the entire battlefield. Another banquet commenced; and every flesh-eating bird and mammal, we believe, feasted for weeks and months. While the banquet of the Lamb and His bride celebrated life and victory, this last "banquet" celebrated death and defeat. Keep in mind that this third coming was preceded by His birth (the first coming) and the general resurrection of the saints (the second coming).

Discussion Questions

1. Who will appear at the judgment seat of Christ?
2. According to the guide, what takes place at the judgment seat?
3. As per the guide, what is the purpose of the crowns believers receive (i.e., what will believers do with them)?
4. Identify the bride and the groom in this chapter.
5. Reread verses 11–21 and briefly put into your own words the real mother of all battles, the battle of Armageddon, and its outcome.

REVELATION 20

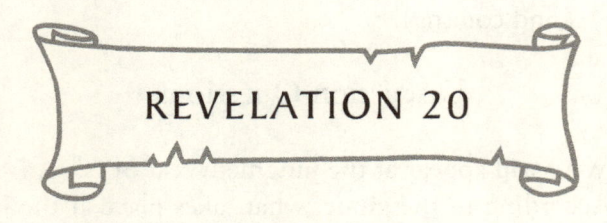

The Millennial Reign of Christ (One Thousand Years)

1Then I saw an angel coming down from heaven, having the key to the bottomless pit and a great chain in his hand. 2He laid hold of the dragon, that serpent of old, who is *the* Devil and Satan, and bound him for a thousand years; 3and he cast him into the bottomless pit, and shut him up, and set a seal on him, so that he should deceive the nations no more till the thousand years were finished. But after these things he must be released for a little while.

4And I saw thrones, and they sat on them, and judgment was committed to them. Then *I saw* the souls of those who had been beheaded for their witness to Jesus and for the word of God, who had not worshiped the beast or his image, and had not received *his* mark on their foreheads or on their hands. And they lived and reigned with Christ for a thousand years. 5But the rest of the dead did not live again until the thousand years were finished. This *is* the first resurrection.

6Blessed and holy *is* he who has part in the first resurrection. Over such the second death has no power, but they shall be priests of God and of Christ, and shall reign with Him a thousand years.

7Now when the thousand years have expired, Satan will be released from his prison 8and will go out to deceive the nations which are in the four corners of the earth, Gog and Magog, to gather them together to battle, whose number *is* as the sand of the sea. 9They went up on the breadth of the earth and surrounded the camp of the saints and the beloved city. And fire came down from God out of heaven and devoured them. 10The devil, who deceived them, was cast into the lake of fire and brimstone where the beast and the false prophet *are*. And they will be tormented day and night forever and ever.

11Then I saw a great white throne and Him who sat on it, from whose face the earth and the heaven fled away. And there was found no place for them. 12And I saw the dead, small and great, standing before God, and books were opened. And another book was opened, which is *the Book of Life*. And the dead were judged according to their works, by the things which were written in the books. 13The sea gave up the dead who were in it, and Death and Hades delivered up the dead who were in them. And they were judged, each one according to his works. 14Then Death and Hades were cast into the lake of fire. This is the second death. 15And anyone not found written in the Book of Life was cast into the lake of fire.

The Binding of Satan

Satan was seized, and John saw a great angel coming down from heaven. He had in his possession a key and a great chain by which he captured Satan, bound him, and locked him in solitary confinement in the bottomless pit. The primary purpose of this was so that he would have no influence over what was about to happen, namely, the thousand-year reign of our Lord Jesus Christ.

We are hearing quite a bit these days about a monstrous atom smasher located in Switzerland. In this collider, they are grappling with dark matter in the universe. In fact, scientists claim that two-thirds of the universe is made up of dark matter. For a long time, we have heard about black or dark holes whose gravity cannot be measured. Is it possible that the bottomless pit was an ancient black hole that had been renovated or converted into a prison for Satan and the others? From this place of solitary confinement, the evil one would be shut down for a while, in fact for one thousand years. During this millennial reign, Christ Jesus would reign from the ancient city of Jerusalem with a group of selected saints.

The Selected Saints

Without any preparation, John was told, "Thrones were given to them and they will judge and reign with Christ for a thousand years" (Revelation 20:4–). Who were these saints? It is now fairly clear to me that the little group found under the golden altar in heaven in chapter 6 made up the beginning of the 144,000 saints. As has been indicated before in chapter 7, that group was selected and sealed with the mark of God. In chapter 14, we met them on Mount Zion in heaven standing with the Lamb. We now know who this group is before us. They are the 144,000 saints who had just arrived from heaven on white horses with the Messiah King to silence Satan and the False Prophet and to begin the thousand-year reign. We now know that they were all beheaded. We also know that they were Jewish believers serving God and the Lamb, and these along with the twelve Old Testament patriarchs (the heads of the twelve tribes of Israel) and the New Testament apostles would rule with Christ throughout the millennial reign. This explains why the Lamb chose only Jewish believers for this grand "experiment."

Someone will say, "Where is the documentation for having the twelve patriarchs and the twelve apostles serving during the millennial reign of Christ?" My answer is that the documentation is found in the fact that both groups were honored in the eternal state. The twelve patriarchs had the twelve tribes of Israel named after them, and the twelve gates in the heavenly city were named after them as well. Likewise, the twelve foundations on which the city wall was built were named after the twelve apostles. In addition, when John was called to heaven in Revelation 4, he saw the great throne of God, and around the throne he saw the twenty-four elders sitting on thrones wearing crowns of gold and assisting in worship.

As is indicated, these patriarchs and apostles were called the twenty-four elders, which were their new identity throughout all eternity. It is unthinkable to me that the Messiah would not have these two groups assisting during the great millennial reign. When God did something great in the kingdom, these two groups were present. During the millennial reign of our Lord, these two groups would be assisting the Messiah and giving council to the 144,000 serving as administrators.

Scenario 3
The Rescue of the Human Race

God's rescue of the human race began immediately after the catastrophic fall in the garden of Eden. God's rescue plan involved the sending of the Messiah, in other words, coming to earth Himself in human flesh. The Messiah would come through a special group of people beginning with Abraham and Sarah and their descendants. God chose Abraham and his descendants as a womb for the Messiah, not because they were good, not because they were smarter than anyone else, and certainly not because they were more capable than any other group on the planet. In fact, they were the least capable and the least adequate. It appears they were chosen because they had nothing to offer God but faith and obedience.

For centuries Abraham and his descendants were called Hebrews. The term *ha-Be-ru* means "stray dogs" in the ancient Sumerian language (Dr. Mark Lovelace, professor of archaeology, classroom lecture, 1963). This derogatory term for a group of people who lived on the fringe areas of society was applied to God's chosen people. It meant that they were not committed to any king, god, or political system. As outsiders Abraham and his descendants were called *ha-Be-ru*. But from the inside this little group had committed itself in covenant to the great God of this universe Who had promised in the covenant that it was through them that He would bring forth a Messiah, a Savior to rescue the entire world. After the exile, God's special people came to be known as Jews.

God's rescue plan for the human race came through the Jewish people, and it appears to me it would only be right that only Jewish martyrs should be chosen for this great visual aid that was about to unfold itself in the millennial reign of Christ. In the garden of Eden, Adam and Eve chose another god and another life for themselves. Satan explained to them that the "shift" was no big deal. He argued that they would not really die and that nothing could happen to them that could not be worked out. He calmed their nerves by reminding them that they would know as much as God and be able to solve all the problems by their own wisdom. But from day one God told Adam and Eve and the world that a calamity too great to explain had entered the human race. The only answer was for God and the human race to start over. Nothing short of regeneration and creation made new could bring them back into a right relationship with God. But Satan started a myth, which has continued throughout every generation: all we need is reformation, not regeneration. Satan claimed that men and women are basically and essentially good and all we need is time, education, and training to demonstrate how good we are. Throughout the generations, Satan's myth has been the mantra of the reformers who insist that all the human race needs are the right information, technology, and right freedom, which will recreate a return to the garden of Eden.

Most of our institutions around the world today are committed to this satanic, godless mantra. Most of the leaders and institutions around our entire planet believe that God is too strict and too perfect and that He is too obsessive over His creation. But our grieving Messiah will have none of this because He knows the hearts and minds and ways of His creation. The thousand-year reign of Christ has one central focus, and that is to demonstrate that mankind needs a Savior and not a program of reformation.

The Thousand-Year Reign

The Messiah would reign over the entire earth from His throne in Jerusalem, assisted by the saints. In several places in the Bible, we are told that when the Messiah comes, He will rule the world with a rod of iron. Whatever else this means, it means that portion in the Lord's Prayer where it says "Thy kingdom come. Thy will be done on earth as it is in heaven" will be realized for the first time (Matthew 6:10). It probably means in this context that no votes will be taken on who is in charge.

It is my view that the other participants in this millennial reign were made up of all who were left on earth after the bowls of judgment. Somehow there was a comparatively small group of people who managed to survive without taking the mark of the Beast or the Mark of God but rather declared themselves to be neutral. They declared that this great cosmic battle was not between them and God but between Satan and God over who would rule the universe. It was not their problem but the combatants' problem. They prided themselves in their neutrality. This group that bore neither mark was invited to Jerusalem by the Messiah and were told they were needed to participate in this grand experiment of reclaiming this ruined planet and its ruined environment. They were told that help would come in the form of the curse being lifted from the planet, resulting in the increase of the fertility of the earth by at least tenfold. All the rules were explained to them. The Messiah was in charge, and the 144,000 saints would be His managers or administrators for this great reformation project. In addition, the aforementioned Old and New Testament patriarchs and apostles would serve as advisers to the Messiah. The group taking part in this grand experiment would be required to participate in worship and Bible study on the first day of every week. The Messiah Himself would lead worship, and the 144,000 would conduct a Bible search of the scriptures. Finally, they would be required to attend the great Hebrew festivals held in Jerusalem.

These neutral survivors were all unbelievers representing every nation, tribe, and people group on the planet. Remember that this once beautiful planet, at the beginning of the millennium, would be in total ruin. These earth dwellers in the end times had the daunting task of rebuilding this planet and all its systems under the tutelage and leadership of the Messiah and His managers (the 144,000). This group would be scientists, engineers, and just common folk who were committed to seeing this planet live again and be brought back to its fullest potential. During this period, everybody would work with their heads, hearts, and hands. In the process of time, life would return to what we generally concede as normal. There would be no death, disease, or disturbances. During this one-thousand-year experiment, there would be no greed or self-centeredness; and the mantra of the Beast would truly unfold and would be characterized by peace, prosperity, and progress. Marriage, family, and children would be a centerpiece. Education, technology, industry, and the cultivation of the planet for produce would still be needed. At some point in this recovery, the dreams and promises of the Old Testament prophets would come true when a lion would lie down with the Lamb and children would play over the holes of what were once poisonous snakes. Everyone would go up to Jerusalem and magnify the Lord.

What we are describing here is a true utopia. All the promises made by the prophets concerning the millennial reign would be witnessed and received by the patriarchs, apostles, and 144,000 martyrs. Everything that man's heart longed and yearned for would be provided through hard work and cooperation. Everything that man truly needed would be available. Everything that man needed for fulfillment would be offered by this near-perfect society. Planet earth would be restored to a condition that might rival the first garden.

The Conclusion

When the Messiah declared that the time was right and the project was declared a success, the final test would be made. The dungeon door in the bottomless pit would swing open, the great chain would fall off, and Satan would be released from prison for a short while. Those living during this grand experiment had lived in a perfect society. Everything they had ever wanted or needed was made available. In the meantime, Satan had had one thousand years to mull over his final response and his last set of actions. Within weeks or months, he had enlisted a massive army of God haters and Christ rejecters to join him in one last effort to defeat God's Messiah and depose God from His throne. How on earth could Satan find such a massive group of people so quickly who wanted to be set free from the Messiah's control and presence?

The great experiment was a demonstration that a "perfect environment" does not produce a perfect or even a good person. A perfect environment does not cure an evil heart. The entire purpose of the millennial reign was designed to show the proof of this statement.

God gave to these earth dwellers a perfect environment on planet earth, including everything that mankind could need or desire. Nothing was held back and certainly not a Savoir, the Messiah Himself, Who ruled in Jerusalem. If what modern man claims is true, then everyone who took part in this grand millennial experiment should have been transformed into saints with pure hearts. But the very opposite took place. As soon as Satan was released from his prison, earth's population who had been raised in a state of perfection flocked to Satan's cause. His cause and goal were to dethrone God, reject His Messiah, and establish himself on the throne of the universe.

Most of you know the rest of the story. Fire rained out of heaven and consumed this massive piece of humanity. Satan was seized and thrown into Hell with his cohorts in crime, the Beast and the False Prophet, never to be released and never to escape from that torment.

The Great White Throne

Every person who ever lived on planet earth who had reached the age of accountability and rejected Christ was summoned in this scene to the great white throne. No one would be left out. No one would be late, and no one would bring along their lawyer. The setting was a heavenly courtroom, and the Lord Jesus Christ was the one in charge. This courtroom would be stripped down to its bare essentials, because everything else had fled away from the presence of the terrifying Messiah Who was King of kings and Lord of lords. At the appropriate time, a massive set of books would be set up in their place, and near them there would be the Book of Life. Just maybe, there would be a massive screen let down and visible to everyone present. Those present would have been raised from the dead and given bodies, which prepared them for eternity. We have partial resurrection of the wicked dead recorded for us in Revelation 14 cast in the language of grapes from the vine of the earth. We are not told when the general resurrection of the wicked would actually take place. Maybe it is alluded to in the words *gave up its dead* or *their dead* (Revelation 20:13). It doesn't matter. The people who belonged here had been summoned and were standing before the Judge. We are told that the sea gave up its dead. In the ancient world, it was thought that those who drowned at sea or lost their lives at sea would be missing forever. No such thing is true. We are also told that death and hades gave up their dead. This is a kind of redundant way of saying that hades gave up all its occupants, since hades was the place where the wicked dead were held in captivity until judgment day. Would there be some kind of gradation in the afterlife for the wicked dead? Everybody in that courtroom would be judged on the basis of their motives, activities, and opportunities they had when they lived on planet earth. All would be asked to explain why they passed up the opportunity of a lifetime and passed over the invitation for salvation and eternal life offered by the redeeming Messiah. I have a feeling that if anybody in that courtroom wanted to argue about why they were there, they would be led to this awesome Book of Life and asked to find their name, which of course they could not. And all those whose names were not found in the Book of Life would be thrown into hell to join company with the most infamous criminals the world had ever known. There would be no paroles, no escapes, and no end to this awesome plight. The worst thing about this place is not going to be heat but separation from God and His Christ and separation from all that was good and all that was worthy. I sincerely believe that the book of Revelation should be the first Bible study taught to young Christians and its revelations should be taught in all courses on evangelism.

Discussion Questions

1. Based on scriptures (verses 2–3), what are the other two names of Satan used in the Revelation?
2. Was Satan destroyed forever when he was thrown into the abyss?
3. According to the guide, briefly describe the purpose of the thousand-year reign of Christ.
4. Discuss any differences between the great white throne judgment (verse 11) and the judgment seat of Christ in the last chapter in terms of who would be judged.
5. In verse 14, discuss the lake of fire and what gets thrown into it and why you think it is called "the second death."

REVELATION 21

The New Jerusalem

1Now I saw a new heaven and a new earth, for the first heaven and the first earth had passed away. Also there was no more sea. 2Then I, John, saw the holy city, New Jerusalem, coming down out of heaven from God, prepared as a bride adorned for her husband. 3And I heard a loud voice from heaven saying, "Behold, the tabernacle of God *is* with men, and He will dwell with them, and they shall be His people. God Himself will be with them *and be* their God. 4And God will wipe away every tear from their eyes; there shall be no more death, nor sorrow, nor crying. There shall be no more pain, for the former things have passed away."

5Then He who sat on the throne said, "Behold, I make all things new." And He said to me, "Write, for these words are true and faithful."

6And He said to me, "It is done! I am the Alpha and the Omega, the Beginning and the End. I will give of the fountain of the water of life freely to him who thirsts. 7He who overcomes shall inherit all things, and I will be his God and he shall be My son. 8But the cowardly, unbelieving, abominable, murderers, sexually immoral, sorcerers, idolaters, and all liars shall have their part in the lake which burns with fire and brimstone, which is the second death."

9Then one of the seven angels who had the seven bowls filled with the seven last plagues came to me and talked with me, saying, "Come, I will show you the bride, the Lamb's wife." 10And he carried me away in the Spirit to a great and high mountain, and showed me the great city, the holy Jerusalem, descending out of heaven from God, 11having the glory of God. Her light *was* like a most precious stone, like a jasper stone, clear as crystal. 12Also she had a great and high wall with twelve gates, and twelve angels at the gates, and names written on them, which are *the names* of the twelve tribes of the children of Israel: 13three gates on the east, three gates on the north, three gates on the south, and three gates on the west.

14Now the wall of the city had twelve foundations, and on them were the names of the twelve apostles of the Lamb. 15And he who talked with me had a gold reed to measure the city, its gates, and its wall. 16The city is laid out as a square; its length is as great as its breadth. And he measured the city with the reed: twelve thousand furlongs. Its length, breadth, and height are equal. 17Then he measured its wall: one hundred *and* forty-four cubits, *according* to the measure of a man, that is, of an angel. 18The construction of its wall was *of* jasper; and the city *was* pure gold, like clear glass. 19The foundations of the wall of the city *were* adorned with all kinds of precious stones: the first foundation *was* jasper, the second sapphire, the third chalcedony, the fourth emerald, 20the fifth sardonyx, the sixth sardius, the seventh chrysolite, the eighth beryl, the ninth topaz, the tenth chrysoprase, the eleventh jacinth, and the twelfth amethyst. 21 The twelve gates *were* twelve pearls: each individual gate was of one pearl. And the street of the city *was* pure gold, like transparent glass.

22 But I saw no temple in it, for the Lord God Almighty and the Lamb are its temple. 23 The city had no need of the sun or of the moon to shine in it, for the glory of God illuminated it. The Lamb *is* its light. 24 And the nations of those who are saved shall walk in its light, and the kings of the earth bring their glory and honor into it. 25 Its gates shall not be shut at all by day (there shall be no night there). 26 And they shall bring the glory and the honor of the nations into it. 27 But there shall by no means enter it anything that defiles, or causes an abomination or a lie, but only those who are written in the Lamb's Book of Life.

All Things Made New

These last two chapters of the Apocalypse are watershed chapters. Along with them come the promises of Jesus as He talked about heaven and our future lives. The apostle Peter (2 Peter 3:10) saw a new heaven and a new earth. The question before us is, What would happen to this present heaven and earth? The apostle Peter told us they would be utterly destroyed by fire.

The reference to a new heaven in this case is pointing to the place where the celestial bodies resided, including deep space. It could well be called the heavenlies. The earth Peter described was new in kind, character, and function. It was not the first earth, the planet on which we live, but it was something completely new. No doubt it was vastly expanded and would rival even the garden of Eden. This new earth would be the place that the saints would call home throughout all eternity. It would be the place where God and the Lamb would take up permanent residence.

But we are left with another important question. What would happen to the wonderful creatures found in the animal kingdom? God had a special place for them on the original earth. Likewise, we have seen them in the millennial reign of Christ on planet earth. In the thousand-year reign of Christ, there were no longer flesh eaters; but instead their food source was made up of grass, fruits, and herbs. It is my view that God would not destroy these wonderful creatures but their eternal home would be a renovated planet somewhere in the universe. In fact, it may require more than one planet to take care of them! No, our animal pets will not be in heaven with us, but they will have all the care they need on a selected planet designed to meet their needs. We will be able to visit these wonderful creatures, including our pets, and continue the relationship we had with them here on earth.

Finally, John saw a new city. Actually it was an old city, an ancient city, that had been relocated. It was the city where God's throne had existed up until this time. This royal city of glory was seen coming down out of heaven like a bride decked out for her husband. When he tried to describe this heavenly and holy city, human speech became inadequate. Words could not bear its weight! It exceeded anything the prophets could describe or the songwriters could compose or even Jesus Himself cared to talk about despite it being His home. This magnificent city, which would have no temple and no external lighting system, would be surrounded by a spectacular wall. The city itself would be 1500 miles cubed, and its wall would have twelve gates, which would represent the twelve Hebrew patriarchs (sons of Jacob). These gates would each be one mammoth pearl. Each gate would be protected by an angel. These twelve angels symbolize security, tranquility, and safety for the people of God throughout all eternity. The wall around the city was built on twelve foundation levels, all of which were aboveground. These twelve foundation levels, or layers, represent the twelve apostles of the New Testament. The building materials would be the most beautiful and costly gems of God's creation. Yes, the streets would be of pure gold as would many of the other structures.

The Perfection of the City

The most important thing about this heavenly city is that the Godhead would dwell there for the rest of eternity. In this city aesthetics and symmetry would find a way to go beyond perfection. In terms of function, we are told the old plagues of the human race—like disease, tears, pain, and sorrow—would flee away. It is my hope that the old common cold would be included in this flight. The most dreaded enemy of all, death, would be thrown into the lake of fire.

Discussion Questions

1. Which verse in this chapter indicates positively that God (Father, Son, and Holy Spirit) will actually live "boots on the ground" with us, His people?
2. Based on Scripture and the guide, is heaven, the New Jerusalem, a real place with dimensions and real materials? If so, what are they?
3. Describe what John wrote about our light source in heaven.

REVELATION 22

The Throne and the Eternal State Began

1And he showed me a pure river of water of life, clear as crystal, proceeding from the throne of God and of the Lamb. 2In the middle of its street, and on either side of the river, *was* the tree of life, which bore twelve fruits, each *tree* yielding its fruit every month. The leaves of the tree *were* for the healing of the nations. 3And there shall be no more curse, but the throne of God and of the Lamb shall be in it, and His servants shall serve Him. 4They shall see His face, and His name *shall be* on their foreheads. 5There shall be no night there: They need no lamp nor light of the sun, for the Lord God gives them light. And they shall reign forever and ever.

6Then he said to me, "These words *are* faithful and true." And the Lord God of the holy prophets sent His angel to show His servants the things which must shortly take place.

7"Behold, I am coming quickly! Blessed *is* he who keeps the words of the prophecy of this book."

8Now I, John, saw and heard these things. And when I heard and saw, I fell down to worship before the feet of the angel who showed me these things.

9Then he said to me, "See *that you do* not *do that.* For I am your fellow servant, and of your brethren the prophets, and of those who keep the words of this book. Worship God." 10And he said to me, "Do not seal the words of the prophecy of this book, for the time is at hand. 11He who is unjust, let him be unjust still; he who is filthy, let him be filthy still; he who is righteous, let him be righteous still; he who is holy, let him be holy still."

12"And behold, I am coming quickly, and My reward *is* with Me, to give to every one according to his work. 13I am the Alpha and the Omega, *the* Beginning and *the* End, the First and the Last."

14Blessed *are* those who do His commandments, that they may have the right to the tree of life, and may enter through the gates into the city. 15But outside *are* dogs and sorcerers and sexually immoral and murderers and idolaters, and whoever loves and practices a lie.

16"I, Jesus, have sent My angel to testify to you these things in the churches. I am the Root and the Offspring of David, the Bright and Morning Star."

17And the Spirit and the bride say, "Come!" And let him who hears say, "Come!" And let him who thirsts come. Whoever desires, let him take the water of life freely.

18For I testify to everyone who hears the words of the prophecy of this book: If anyone adds to these things, God will add to him the plagues that are written in this book; 19and if anyone takes away from the words of the book of this prophecy, God shall take away his part from the Book of Life, from the holy city, and *from* the things which are written in this book.

20He who testifies to these things says, "Surely I am coming quickly."
Amen. Even so, come, Lord Jesus!
21The grace of our Lord Jesus Christ *be* with you all. Amen.

Our Worship

We are told in this last chapter of the Bible what believers ought to be doing until Jesus Christ comes back to take us to heaven. The number one priority as to what we should be doing until Jesus comes back is to worship and glorify Him. Worship is always the priority in the life of a believer. Most of the scenes in the Revelation are about heaven, and every time these scenes are open, we see that the angels and the saints of God re involved in intense worship. Worship is extremely important as we face the end times. When everything around us is coming apart and it appears that nothing can be trusted and that nothing is stable, believers need to know that God and His Son are on the scene and He is in control of history and the goal toward which history is moving.

The opening scene in this last chapter presents a river of living water flowing out from under the throne of God located in the New Jerusalem. While this life-giving water can and should be taken literally, in some places it represents the Holy Spirit in all His abundance. In the Gospel of John, chapter 7, verse 38, on one of the great feast days in Jerusalem, Jesus cried out, "Whoever believes in Me out of his innermost being shall flow rivers of living water." He said this to remind us that He was talking about the spirit.

Of special interest is the statement in verse 2 that declares the leaves of the trees of life (see Ezekiel 47:7) will be used for the healing of the nations. We have already been told that in the eternal state, "there will be no more death or mourning or crying or pain" (Revelation 21:4). Certainly there will be no diseases or infections in heaven. Why then do we need these leaves for the healing of the nations in the eternal state? The answer is I don't know. This is a mystery we will find answers to when we get to heaven.

Our worship in the last days as we approach the end times should lead us and show us the life, personality, and power of the Holy Spirit. True worship enables the spirit of God to fill us and refresh us and bring forth all the resources of heaven. The throne is central in this passage as well, and God's people here on earth should be learning about how to stay before the throne of God.

Watching and Waiting

Between now and the time that Jesus comes back, God's people ought to be involved in watching and waiting for His return. More than one time in this last chapter the Lord tells us He is coming back soon. Many people have questioned Jesus's promise to return soon. The primary purpose for delay on the part of our Lord is not uncertainty but to give us more time to bring as many people to heaven with us as we possibly can. His delay, if we choose to call it that, is really an expression of His great mercy and amazing grace. God is deeply grieved every time a human being rejects His Son and chooses to take the Mark of the Beast. It is a grief that we cannot comprehend. What I am suggesting is that this delay provides us with time to get ready and be prepared. We are to keep our eyes on the signs of the times Jesus said, but more importantly every day should be time used to practice the application of agape (divine) love in every situation. We must learn how to be overcomers through the power of the spirit and to enlarge our capacities for praise and adoration. In order to achieve this heavenly lifestyle, we desperately need the infilling of the Holy Spirit Who provides to us His life without limit and makes available to us everything that God has for us.

Serving Our King

In the past we have always been told that man cannot look upon the face of God and live, but in the eternal state the saints will be able to gaze on the face of God as long as they wish. This is made possible because in the eternal state we will be clothed in our heavenly bodies. The face of God that we will be able to gaze upon is none other than the face of our Lord Jesus Christ. However, in verse 4 of this chapter, a remarkable claim is made. We are told that God's servants will see His face.

Also, in verse 4 we are told that in eternity the saints will have His name written on their foreheads. The name of God appearing on our foreheads in eternity will be the secret name of the Lamb of God. It will be the name mentioned in chapter 19, verse 12, which says, "He has a name written on Him that no one knows but Himself."

Throughout this amazing book, we are challenged to serve the Lord and work in the kingdom. This work is not to earn salvation but to express our salvation with massive gratitude. In this last chapter, we are told that God's servants will serve Him and there will be no place for us to argue about what serving God means. The Pharisee in us should have already been laid to rest a long time ago. Part of our work, and probably the most urgent part, is to be consistently involved in calling people to follow the Lord Jesus Christ. We are told in this chapter that the Holy Spirit and the bride, the church, are calling out for men and women to embrace the Savior. When men and women respond to the Lamb, they are told they must join the great company of believers on earth with the same cry, "Come now, to salvation!" The scripture says it best, "The Spirit and the bride say, 'Come!' And let him who hears say, 'Come!' Whoever is thirsty, let him come; and whoever wishes, let him take the free gift of the water of life" (Revelation 22:17).

LEONARD QUICK, M. DIV.

What a Marvelous Time

We mentioned that Jesus promised to come back soon for those who love Him. This was meant to be a new promise to every new generation of believers and was meant to stimulate, challenge, and excite us to bring as many lost people to heaven as we possibly can. When Jesus comes and time is morphed into eternity, there will be no more grace for unbelievers. What a marvelous time to be living this close to the end of time. What a marvelous time to hear the promises of our Lord in a way that they appear to be addressed directly to us. What a marvelous time to know that all the power and strength we need to be obedient is available in and through the spirit. What a marvelous time to practice and implement the wonderful things we have learned from the Apocalypse.

Discussion Questions

1. What things are mentioned in the first two verses of this chapter that indicate that heaven is indeed a real place?
2. In verses 3–5, discuss further evidence that we will literally get to see the Lord face-to-face and that there will be no need for the sun.
3. According to verses 12–16 (and the guide), why should we be concerned about our friends and loved ones who may not know Jesus personally?
4. Based on verses 18–19, what are the consequences of adding to or changing in any way the contents of "this book"? Discuss the possibility of this book meaning the whole Bible as well.
5. Based on chapter 1, verse 3, what promise does God make to those who read and heed (obey/keep) the words of the book of Revelation? As in the previous question, could this book in this verse also include the whole Bible?

REVELATION GLOSSARY

Apocalypse/apocalyptic. The book of Revelation makes use of coded language. The terms *apocalypse* and *apocalyptic* can be translated as that which is uncovered or revealed, hence the term *revelation*.

The seven lampstands. Represent the seven churches of Asia Minor.

The seven stars and seven angels. Represent the pastors of the seven churches of Asia Minor.

Asia Minor—Now the territory of modern-day Turkey.

The four living creatures. Symbolize everything that breathes and lives on planet earth, including human beings.

The twenty-four elders. Represent the twelve patriarchs of the Old Testament who were the leaders of the twelve tribes of Israel and the twelve New Testament apostles.

The seven flaming lamps. Represent the Holy Spirit.

The sea of glass. The seas and oceans represent chaos, turmoil, and unrest. In heaven John saw a sea not of water but of glass. This sea of glass in heaven tells us that there is no chaos, turmoil, unrest, or danger. In chapter 21, verse 1b, the Word says, "There was no more sea."

The scroll and the seven seals. The scroll and the seals describe the historical and spiritual events that make up the last seven years of human history on planet earth.

The small group under the altar. This group was the nucleus of the 144,000 who would play a critical role in the millennial reign of Christ.

Hades. The Greek word for the place where the unbelieving dead reside until the day of judgment occurs.

The 144,000. This group is comprised of 144,000 Jewish believers who followed the Lamb.

The seven trumpets. The trumpet blasts indicate a second and more intense wave of judgment and punishment upon unbelievers.

The two olive trees and the two lampstands. These two lampstands represent the light of the gospel, and the olive trees provide the olive oil, which represents the Holy Spirit.

The two great signs. A sign symbolizes a window through which one can see what God is doing in the world.

The woman. Represents the nation or at least the remnant of Israel.

The offspring of the woman. Symbolize born-again Jewish believers.

The Dragon. Symbolizes Satan.

War in heaven. This conflict actually took place in space-time.

The Beast. This is the first beast, which is referred to by some as the Antichrist who is actually Satan's son. This Beast came up (appeared) out of the sea, which means out of chaos, confusion, and conflict.

The False Prophet. Came up out of the earth, which represents a stable environment, which is seen as a worldwide religious organization.

The Image. A prefect clone of the first Beast.

The Mark of the Beast. This mark might well be a secret name that the Beast will force his followers to receive on the forehead as a means of obedience and giving them access to trade.

666. In Jewish thought represents unredeemed man. When it is raised to the third power, it describes a person totally controlled by evil.

Two great reapings. The reaping of the church is Jesus's favorite term for the resurrection of saints by a selected group of angels; this is followed by the reaping of the wicked.

The third great sign (Revelation 15:1). The seven bowls of undiluted wrath of God, poured out on unbelieving humanity.

The judgment seat of Christ. This event took place just before the wedding of Christ and the church and the wedding banquet in chapter 19.

The numerology (numbers in Revelation). Theologians and commentators differ immensely on the meaning of the imagery and numbers in this book. The following numbers and their meanings are only the author's ideas and suggestions:

- 2—Witnesses (observers) and/or caretakers of the gospel.
- 3—Unity, accomplishment, Trinity.
- 3 1/2—Half of seven (perfection), which represents precariousness and disruption.
- 4—Whole world, all of nature; worldwide universality.
- 5—Represents a short period of time, the actual lifespan of locusts (Revelation 9:5), salvation or judgment.
- 6—This number represents unredeemed man; three sixes together (666) represent the Antichrist who is absolute evil.
- 7—The favorite number in Jewish thought, which represents perfection and completeness; God's number, sovereign perfection.
- 12—Represents completeness, perfection, fullness (Revelation 21:12).
- 24—The leadership of God's people (Revelation 4:4).
- 666—The Mark of the Beast, Satan's number, represents the cursed.
- 1000 (Revelation 20:2)—Magnitude, fullness; those reserved for God; the golden age.
- 144,000 (Revelation 7:4)—Fullness of the community of believers throughout time and space.
- 200,000,000—Two myriads of myriads, i.e., the largest conceivable gathering of people.

ABOUT THE AUTHOR

Leonard C. Quick grew up in Southeast Georgia where he currently lives. He graduated from Mercer University with a BA degree and from Southeastern Baptist Theological Seminary with an MDiv. He has pastored churches for fifty years and served with his wife, Betty, as missionaries for two years with the International Mission Board of the Southern Baptist Convention in Rio de Janeiro, Brazil.

Leonard and Betty have three sons and a daughter, twelve grandchildren, and sixteen great-grandchildren.

CPSIA information can be obtained
at www.ICGtesting.com
Printed in the USA
BVHW071039200223
658843BV00006B/289